Why You Can't Stay Silent

A Biblical Mandate to Shape Our Culture

FOCUS ON THE FAMILY®

Why You Can't Stay Silent

A Biblical Mandate to Shape Our Culture

TOM MINNERY

Tyndale House Publishers, Inc.
Wheaton, Illinois

WHY YOU CAN'T STAY SILENT: A BIBLICAL MANDATE TO SHAPE OUR CULTURE
Copyright © 2001 by Tom Minnery, Focus on the Family. All rights reserved.
International copyright secured.

Library of Congress Cataloging-in-Publication Data
Minnery, Tom.
   Why you can't stay silent : a biblical mandate to shape our culture / by Tom Minnery.
      p. cm.
Includes bibliographical references and index.
   ISBN 1-56179-925-4
1. Church and the world. I.Title.
BR115.W6 M453 2001
261'.0973—dc21

2001005648

A Focus on the Family Book published by Tyndale House Publishers, Wheaton, Illinois.

Editor: Ray Seldomridge
Front cover design: Lovgren Marketing Group

Printed in the United States of America

02 03 04/10 9 8 7 6 5 4 3

For Dr. James Dobson—
boss, friend, and colaborer in a sometimes
rocky corner of the Lord's vineyard

———

CONTENTS

ACKNOWLEDGMENTS

Thanks to the publishing team at Focus on the Family for encouraging me in this project: Kurt Bruner, Al Janssen, Larry Weeden, Jane Terry, and particularly Ray Seldomridge, whose meticulous care and attention to these pages improved them immensely.

Thanks to my wife, Deb, and children, Dave, Jen, and Beth, who saw me even less than usual and understood why. Thanks especially to Beth for lending me her skills with the bibliography and appendices.

And finally, thanks to my friend Dave Watson, who said, "Writing a book? Why don't you use my laptop?"

PROLOGUE

I have always loved New York City. When I was a newspaper reporter, I spent a lot of time there. I grew fascinated by its problems, its polyglot population, its insane traffic, and its frenetic, 24-hour vitality.

From time to time I have traveled there on business for Focus on the Family, and as it happened I had an appointment in New York just a week after the terrible terrorist attack on the World Trade Center. After I arrived in Manhattan, I did what I usually do when I have an evening open. I walked to the discount theatre booth on Times Square to see whether any worthwhile shows were available. On that particular evening, nearly every show was half price, so few were the theatergoers in New York that week. I had my pick.

Still, I didn't go to any show that night. Instead I hopped aboard a subway train for lower Manhattan. I had something else to do. I wanted to visit the site of the World Trade Center wreckage, to get as close as I could, to stand there and brood. I wanted to do this for the same reason that people go to funeral homes—just to be close in a time of crisis.

But I didn't know how close I would be able to get. I was surprised to see that the Canal Street subway station in the vicinity of the Trade towers was still open. I left the train at that point and began walking. I passed police who were patrolling every block, and although the streets had been closed to civilian auto traffic, no one seemed bothered by me.

As I got closer I could make out ahead a harsh white glare. It came from dozens of portable lights that had been erected at the crash site, the kind used for illuminating highway construction projects at night. I was getting close to the staging area for the huge rescue effort that had already been underway for a week. Still, no one seemed to notice me, so I pressed on.

In a few more moments I found myself in the middle of an eerie halogen city. I was surrounded by rescue teams, medical paraphernalia, and earth-moving equipment. Just beyond, still two blocks away, there loomed above the street one part of the huge pile of debris that had once been the World Trade Center.

Here is where I stopped. If I kept going I would only get in someone's way, and the scene before me was difficult enough to absorb. I was on the set of a disaster movie, only there was no movie.

I milled around among crowds of dirty, tired firefighters coming and going from the recovery site. All around were squads of police, FBI agents, and military people in battle fatigues. The soldiers were positioned in the intersection directing the constant flow of traffic in and out of the site—dump trucks, emergency vehicles, police cars, and shiny black government security vehicles. This hubbub, this crush of people and traffic, was so familiar in Manhattan. But the makeup of this crowd and its grim purpose were something the city had never seen before on this scale.

My own emotional reaction to all of this was one that I would never have predicted, one that I still can't fully sort out. I was moved by the somber scene and fascinated by the buzz of activity. But I was also taken by the plain fact that I was surrounded by abundance. I was in the middle of a land of plenty.

I was surrounded by platoons of rescue workers, all of them thoroughly equipped for their grim task. I had seen rows and rows of portable electric generators, all new, all still wrapped in plastic. I had walked past heavy skid loads of bottled water, past more food tents than I had ever seen at a state fair, and past stack upon stack of five-gallon plastic buckets. These were used for careful removal of small amounts of debris to be sifted for clues of lost loved ones—a tooth, a belt buckle, the remains of a wallet. I saw piles of spare respirators, shovels, hard hats, gloves, and boots. I also saw stacks of stretchers for use in bearing out the wounded, though tragically none would be needed.

I felt that all these people and all this equipment and all these supplies were abundant for the need at hand. This rescue site was a full-scale city of industry, splendidly equipped for round-the-clock production.

Something else was in abundance in those somber days following the terrorist attack on New York, something evident everywhere, something one didn't need to journey all the way to Ground Zero to find. For the first time in a long while in America, God was in abundance in our public life.

In the days following the tragedy, the president invoked the name of

God reverently and constantly, both in his formal speeches and his informal presentations. In an unprecedented scene, nearly half of the Congress, who had gathered at the Capitol in a show of press conference unity, spontaneously broke into a stanza of "God Bless America."

All across the country, churches held special services to pray for America and her leaders, as well as to mourn the dead. The crowds at these services were large. On the Sunday following the Tuesday tragedy, church attendance swelled again. For some years now the nation has recognized a National Day of Prayer, but in the days following the terrorist attack we saw something new—a spontaneous national week of prayer.

To be sure, some of this was thin and shallow God talk. But we live in a day in which the ACLU can file a lawsuit against a moment of silence in a public school, absurdly claiming that even this pointed lack of expression amounts to an unconstitutional establishment of religion. Let us celebrate what we can get.

There was something else about this reverence for God. It arrived wrapped in red, white, and blue. Patriotism surged—not the yellow-ribbon-'round-the-ole-oak-tree sentimentality we have seen before, but a firm swell of pride in America. This was born out of concern that she had sustained a blow to vital parts and out of determined confidence that she would rise to this new challenge.

Reverence for God and pride in country are two virtues sniffed at by many, thought to be relics of the past, now gone for good in our postmodern, post-Christian, post-everything-that-is-decent America.

But there they were, still intact. It was like arriving home from vacation and finding the garden still growing when we thought that surely the weeds or the rabbits had conquered it while we were away.

Proper care in the spring is why gardens survive summer's neglect. Reverence for God surfaced because it was planted and nourished by earlier generations of Americans, though not by our own. We've allowed the garden to languish. In our day we've been cowed by the forces of secularism, and we've been content to worship God safely within the four walls of churches while allowing the larger society to go to seed. Our country has been vital because it has been moral, and we've sensed that the vitality has ebbed away in our generation.

The neglect must stop. Our generation must cultivate morality anew for generations to come. I trust that you believe this, too. That is why you have picked up this book. That is why you can't stay silent.

—TOM MINNERY
Colorado Springs
October 2001

INTRODUCTION

I'm in a hearing room at a federal building in Miami, and I'm smoldering inside. To my left sits an editor for Penthouse *magazine, a man with whom I've struck up a ... what, exactly? Not a friendship, but an odd congeniality. We've often been together. We have debated the subject of pornography in private and in public many times, and I know his arguments as well as he knows mine. But I haven't been able to convince him of anything, least of all the reasons for my Christian faith. On this day, as we sit together in this room, the very presence of this man reminds me of my failure to make a dent in his smugness, let alone in his life.*

To my left sit two sharply dressed lawyers. They represent one of the country's most vicious men. He publishes rancid pornography, is long since a millionaire, and pays each of these attorneys more in two hours than I make in a week. In front of me, at a witness table, is a 16-year-old girl in tears, telling in graphic detail about when she was 10 and a neighbor man, a close family friend, made her do to him the things he showed her in pornographic magazines. Her parents would hate her if she told, he said. So she didn't. But after years of this, she did go to another neighbor, a doctor, who responded by molesting her also. The experience destroyed her soul. By age 13 she tried to kill herself but failed, and now, with years of intense psychiatric help, she's trying to kill the shame. While this teen is talking, I hear a noise behind me and turn around. It's a reporter from a major newspaper. He is snickering.

The topic of pornography was my introduction to social activism. In 1985 I was editing a book for people who wanted to learn how to fight it. I closely followed the work of the Attorney General's Commission on Pornography, which spent a year slogging through a sewer of human tragedy. Their assignment was to make sense of it all for a report to Congress.

That morning, sitting in that squalid hearing, I wasn't taking very good notes. I wanted to start throwing chairs at people. And here I go again. I'm smoldering as I write these words.

Actually, the commission blew a crater in the crusted world of hard-core pornography. It recommended many changes in law to Congress, and every one of those changes was made. The administration of (the senior) President George Bush fought obscenity hard, and big-time porno kings went to jail. But then, with the arrival of the Clinton administration, a new wind blew and the crater silted over. The pipeline of prosecutions emptied, and no pornographer anywhere had much to worry about.

Because libertines in the Clinton Justice Department did absolutely nothing about adult, hard-core pornography—most of it plainly illegal—a new era of depravity arose with the arrival of Internet technology. Worse swill than anything that had ever landed a porno king in prison lay only a few clicks away from any eight-year-old kid with a computer. The *Adult Video News* eventually wrote about how wonderful it was to be in the porno business, now that the feds were looking the other way.

Is this how things are supposed to be? Are people like you and me, people who care, destined to be disappointed? Is everything simply going to get worse and worse? Sometimes it seems there's a glimmer of hope, as when the Pornography Commission report was taken seriously. But soon hope was dashed, and—let's admit it—that's the way things usually wind up. People in public authority can ignore immense problems, and nobody does anything about it.

Let's cut right to the ultimate question: What would Jesus do about all of this? Would He stand quietly on the sidelines of societal decay and speak only about the next world, ignoring this one? Surely His heart would grieve with the 16-year-old girl who bravely testified at the Miami hearing. But what would He *do* about the sexual disgraces that brought her to ruin? More to the point, what would He want us, His followers, to do about all of this?

It's a complicated question, *what Jesus would do*. And 10 years prior to the day I sat in that Miami hearing room, ready to throw a chair at the cackling reporter, I never would have thought to ask it. That guy got under my skin because I recognized his cynical attitude. I used to have it myself. I used to be one of those reporters.

It took me several weeks in the autumn of 1975 just to get over the giddiness of leaving my office in the National Press Building each day and heading to the U.S. Capitol. It's a graceful and grand building, the source of so much history. I was a newly promoted Capitol Hill correspondent for Gannett Newspapers, the country's largest chain, and I was fascinated to observe firsthand how Washington works, to chronicle the clash of opposing political forces in the elusive pursuit of something called "the good of the country." I wrote about the bright newcomers trying to make names for themselves, and about the self-serving fools who were squandering the reputations they had already earned.

Meanwhile, my wife, Deb, and I were "newcomers" of another sort. Just before moving to Washington from Rochester, New York, we had begun to take our faith seriously and build a relationship with Jesus Christ. Now, at a church near our new home, I was stunned when the pastor asked me to teach the book of First Peter to an adult Sunday school class. I accepted the challenge. I remember clearly the first time I read through the first chapter of that short letter, sitting home one evening at the desk in our living room. I was shocked. I had never read anything so profound.

But I also had a lot of questions about those first few sentences. And there was only one place I knew to get answers—the public library. Next day, instead of eating lunch, I dashed from my office to the D.C. public library. I checked out some books on First Peter, and that night I got up from my desk, carried my Bible downstairs, and said to Deb, "You know, if even 10 percent of this book is true, it could change your life!" And indeed, it was about to change ours.

The giddiness with my job didn't last. Gradually, the stately old Capitol became just another place to work, and then the cynicism crept in. I remember exactly how it began. It was Inauguration Day 1977, the day Jimmy Carter took the oath of office as president. I was assigned to write a feature story about the people who didn't care, the folks sitting in restaurants and walking about near, but not at, the inauguration. I thought it was a dumb assignment, but there it was. My interview subjects were to be ordinary people for whom the sitting of a new president meant absolutely nothing. And I found them—people drinking in taverns, eating alone at lunch counters, walking their dogs in a nearby park, all perfectly oblivious to the great ceremony on the Capitol steps and the subsequent parade down Pennsylvania Avenue to the White House. I found no one with anything particularly insightful to tell me; they had seen it all before, or their man hadn't won, or they couldn't get off work. Most of them, though, just shrugged. They didn't seem to know why none of it mattered.

I was surprised at how many newspapers around the country used my story, some of them on their front pages. Editors seemed to care a lot about people who didn't care at all. Perhaps their judgment that day betrayed their own cynicism, which is a common trait in newspeople, and I shouldn't have been surprised when it took root in me. Gradually I began to be less moved by the business of lawmaking, the lurch and jerk of shifting alliances, the mismatch of principle and pragmatism, the monumental struggle to accomplish anything in the name of the people. I began to tell myself that I didn't want to stay there much longer. I wanted out. My four years as a reporter in Washington provided a useful education, but I'd had enough.

Simultaneously, my study of First Peter proceeded, and I made more lunchtime dashes to the New Testament shelves of the library. My hunger to learn more about God's Word grew and grew. I began wanting to study it seriously and praying about what that might mean. Finally, one day, I told Deb I wanted to attend seminary. To my surprise, she was overjoyed. She showed me her prayer list, and I saw she had been praying that I would leave the newspaper business and enter a Christian ministry full-time. I applied to Dallas Theological Seminary and was accepted (although I eventually finished my studies at Trinity Evangelical Divinity School near Chicago). We sold our house, packed up our household and two toddlers, and left Washington.

In Texas my desire to learn about faith, theology, and the Bible grew intense and deep. I found myself readily replacing the cynicism of Washington with the richness of graduate theological studies.

But a curious thing happened during my year at Dallas Seminary. I was sitting on a lunchtime discussion panel about media and religion, along with several other people who were knowledgeable about the news business. One of them, a member of the seminary public relations staff, was named Peggy Wehmeyer. Shortly thereafter, she told me she had received an opportunity to leave the seminary and take a job as an on-air television reporter at one of the network affiliates in Dallas. Normally, TV reporters work for years to make it to a big market like Dallas, but Peggy had been given the chance to start a career there. She wanted to know whether I thought this was a good idea.

I found Peggy to be articulate, intelligent, and well grounded in the faith. I thought she would make a terrific reporter. And what a refreshing change it would be to have an evangelical on television news! I suggested that she pursue it, and she did.

Peggy fared so well that in 1994 she was hired by Peter Jennings, the ABC anchorman, to become for seven years the only religion reporter on any of the national news programs. Imagine that—the only network religion reporter, and a learned, serious-minded evangelical Christian. Every time I've mentioned Peggy to people unfamiliar with her, they've become excited that someone with her credentials could occupy such an influential position.

Here is why I find all of this curious. While Deb and I were attending our church in suburban Washington, D.C., and while we were in seminary in Dallas, not once did anyone encourage me to continue in secular journalism and to consider it a worthy mission field. It didn't seem to occur to anyone that a Christian in a large, secular newspaper organization might be strategically placed to accomplish good. Deb and I listened to many sermons in which people were called to consider "full-time Christian service," but this service was always understood to mean work in the pastorate or the foreign mission field or a Christian agency of some sort. I might have considered returning to the secular world after my seminary studies if someone had suggested it to me.

Any church today would jump at the opportunity to invite Peggy Wehmeyer as a guest speaker. They would appreciate hearing her describe the challenge she faced in being a Christian and fairly reporting Christian activities from such an important platform. If she were still in that job, no one would be asking her to consider leaving ABC News for "full-time Christian service."

We Christians are an inconsistent people. We admire a believer who occupies a worldly role of great influence, for we see there is much good that can be accomplished for God's kingdom in such a place. At the same time, we are very willing to call Christians out of the world into "full-time Christian service," even if it means no more than calling them into the Christian subculture where they have fewer contacts with secular people.

There is confusion afoot these days about the world and the Christian's place in it. Are we guerrilla fighters, sneaking behind enemy lines to plant a few tracts and snatch a few converts, hustling them back into the friendly confines of our congregations, but otherwise disdaining the world and all it represents and hoping only for the quick return of Christ? Or is there another role for us? Are we to be in the world, not hiding who we are, but boldly defending what we believe and inviting others to consider the claims of Christ?

Are we leaven hidden in the loaf, or are we light unshielded by any bushel?

Are we salt made to be rubbed into a decaying culture for the purpose of preservation?

What does it mean to be "in the world and not of it" and to be salt and light?

What happens when being those things means raising uncomfortable issues that make the gospel message controversial in the eyes of those who need it most?

Is there a way to do it without needlessly creating enemies?

Finally, what can one person do in the face of so many problems?

These are no small questions, and they are the subject of this book.

Part One

SHOULDN'T SOMEBODY DO SOMETHING?

CHAPTER ONE

When You Can't Stay Silent

SOME YEARS AGO I SERVED AS MODERATOR of our Baptist church board. Election day was drawing near, and our state had changed the law to make it easier for people to register to vote. No longer did it have to be done at the county clerk's office. The convenient new mail-in system meant that anyone with a stack of forms and a table and chair could register people. I thought it would be nice to set up a table at church on Sunday morning, so I proposed the idea at our next board meeting.

Wow! Silence. I might as well have suggested that we paint the parking lot in polka dots. The idea simply didn't compute. Finally the pastor said something: "I don't think so; it sounds worldly to me. The church probably shouldn't be involved in that." And that, as it turned out, was the high point of his argument. I pressed the matter, but the pastor didn't have much more to say, and neither did anyone else. There were a few never-done-it-that-way-befores; no one had given this idea much thought, and no one cared to.

That was 20 years ago, and culture has slid a long way since then. All about us we see evidence that our country's moral heritage is receding like the tide. And when the tide recedes, the rocks lie exposed. As that common moral consensus ebbs away, wouldn't one expect the rock of Christ's church—the believing remnant—to stand exposed, prominent, and unmovable, a force to be reckoned with? Would the guys on my church board at least be willing to let me set up my voter registration table today?

I don't think so. At the very time when the moral authority of informed Christian citizens seems to be desperately needed, there are powerful voices urging Christian people to burrow deeper into the sand, to stay undercover, to mute what might otherwise become a thunderous voice of moral righteousness.

Why Government Can't Save You reads the title of a book by one of the country's most recognized Bible teachers, John MacArthur. He argues that Christians cannot force others to accept their views, that God has not called us to declare war on our culture, and that our task is to obey our government, whatever it tells us to do. But in fact, is the book title true? About the time it was published, the United States Supreme Court also published something. It was a decision, by a one-vote, 5-4 majority, that said Nebraska's law against partial-birth abortion was unconstitutional. Thus thousands of late-term unborn children, fully viable and fully born except for their heads, are going to be killed in the most gruesome manner imaginable—by having their brains sucked out. Change one vote on that court, and government would literally be saving thousands from what can only be described as infanticide. Yes, in certain situations, government can indeed save you.

Two other Christian leaders, who at one time were prominent lieutenants of Jerry Falwell in his Moral Majority days, have turned against their old ways and their former boss. Now, they not only warn Christians against taking on the culture, but they have gone a step further by indicting those who do, in the very title of their book: *Blinded by Might.* Cal Thomas and Ed Dobson claim that Christians who work for moral laws are actually hungry for worldly power and are foolishly trying to impose Christian values from the top. "Trickle-down morality" will not work, they say, and like MacArthur, they contend that culture can only be changed "one heart at a time."

One of the authors, Cal Thomas, has used a laugh line in some of his speeches that mocks Christians who, he says, believe "righteousness will arrive on Air Force One." It's his way of saying exactly what MacArthur's book title says, that people waste their time when they turn to government to solve moral problems. But wasn't it a president who, by the stroke of a pen, freed millions of slaves? And a century later, wasn't it another president who ordered federal attorneys and then federal troops into the South to break the back of racial segregation? Didn't still other presidents appoint Supreme Court justices who found a constitutional right for mothers to kill their nearly born children?

Is it possible that the highly "secular" institution of government has something very important to do with morality? And if that's true, might it then follow that Christians have a reason to pay attention to what government does? The fact is, when hearts are changed by the gospel, sometimes those hearts begin to beat in new rhythms. These are the people who, renewed in Christ, begin to see with fresh eyes what is wrong, because the gospel has taught them what is right. They are the ones who cannot ignore what is happening around them, the ones who stand up and say, "Somebody has to do something!"

PEOPLE WHO DO SOMETHING

One of these people is a Vermont sheep farmer named Tom Wilson.

Wilson suffers no delusions about what government can and can't accomplish. He was an Army captain and served two tours of duty in Vietnam. He won a Bronze Star for heroism during a rocket attack against the city of Banmethuot, a U.S. stronghold in the central highlands. Although Wilson's government recognized his military contribution, the rest of his country didn't seem to, and the virulent antiwar protests made no sense to Wilson upon his return home. Disgusted by government, he retreated to a 160-acre farm to raise his sheep, his apples, and his family. And that, pretty much, has been that for Tom Wilson ever since.

But government has a way of not leaving you alone, and when decent people like Tom Wilson stop paying attention, government can grow aggressive and intrusive and do things that take your breath away. That's just what the Vermont State Legislature did when, with its collective arm twisted hard by a left-leaning State Supreme Court, it passed a bill granting every privilege of marriage to same-sex couples. The campaign for and against the civil union bill was ugly, with reporters crawling all over Vermont and residents pitted one against another.

It was too much for Wilson; he could no longer ignore the exasper-
ating events in Montpelier. In his mind, marriage mirrors clearly the relationship between Christ and His church, and for the state government
to besmirch that sacred union was enough to bring him off his farm. At
age 56, Tom Wilson became a grassroots Christian activist.

After the governor signed the legislature's bill into law, Wilson tele-
phoned seven of his neighbors. They gathered at one of the homes for a
discussion, not just about the same-sex civil union bill but also about the
larger scope of the homosexual agenda—redefining the family and
indoctrinating schoolchildren with the belief that homosexuality is normal and acceptable. At the second meeting, 15 people came, and by the
third one, nearly a hundred people showed up. Fortunately, Wilson had
seen the need and scheduled it for the Topsham Town Hall. Wilson's pastor asked him to set up yet another meeting, this one in Barre. He did,
and 75 people came, remarkable for a town of only 9,538.

The meetings spread, and before long a hundred groups had organized themselves across the state. In an interview, Wilson said, "Some
people thought the idea of cell groups was Leninist or communist. That's
not the idea I had. It's more like mitosis [the growth of an organism
through the division of single cells], like bones with the sinews and flesh
being laid on. It's the Body of Christ."[1] Thus was born in Vermont a
movement called simply "Take Back Vermont." The name came from a
cattle farmer, Richard Lambert of Graniteville, who declared that civil
unions were the last straw, and it was time to act.

And that's all it could be called: a movement. It never incorporated
or officially organized. Nonetheless, its spare, even bleak-looking black-
and-white signs began sprouting up across the state and then the nation,
via print and broadcast reporters who had come to Vermont from all over
to report on the campaign against civil unions. The movement's purpose
was simple: to find those friends and neighbors who were opposed to
civil unions, and to be sure they were registered to vote in the fall when
the legislators who had passed the civil union bill, and the governor who
had signed it into law, were up for reelection.

"Take Back Vermont" rumbled through the political landscape. In
the November election, 17 legislators who voted for the civil union bill

were defeated, and that cataclysm put Republicans in charge of the lower house of the legislature for the first time in 14 years. In the state senate, the Democratic party's narrow hold on the majority was shaved even finer, and the governor who signed the bill barely escaped with his political life. It wasn't the complete housecleaning they had hoped for, but it was enough for round one. The grassroots rebellion called "Take Back Vermont" shows no signs of dissipating, as its people have turned their attention to other elections down the road.

In Vermont that year, lots of people spoke and lots of legislators were suddenly out of work. Newcomers to the political process, or people who had been neglecting to pay attention to that process, found their voice with the help of the farmer who left his flock and his apple orchard and organized the uprising in the name of a godly principle—the sanctity of marriage.

Wilson's pastor, Neal Laybourne of Barre Evangelical Free Church, was the one who urged him forward, fully confident that a political protest movement was an act of righteousness consistent with Scripture. He takes direction from Paul's writing in 2 Corinthians 10:3-4a, which starts by saying: "For though we live in the world, we do not wage war as the world does. The weapons we fight with are not the weapons of the world."

"That," Pastor Laybourne says, "is where a lot of people stop and say we shouldn't stand for righteousness in the public square. But then you read in verse five: 'We demolish arguments and every pretension that sets itself up against the knowledge of God, and we take captive every thought to make it obedient to Christ.'

"The church must be a public voice for the eternal truths of God," Laybourne says, and he believes pastors should show the way.[2]

THE CANNONBALLS FROM WABASH

There are a thousand Tom Wilsons in the country today, people who have been smacked in the face with a problem and start from nowhere to solve it. They are armed only with a deep conviction that a wrong has

been done and that somebody ought to do something about it. Sometimes it's a problem started by an errant government policy, as in Vermont, and sometimes it's a problem in the culture, a problem having
absolutely nothing to do with government.

When two mothers, Bonnie Fleming and Brenda Ingraham of
Wabash, Indiana, visited their local Hook's Drug Store one day in 1988,
they noticed a new magazine on the rack, a publication called *Sassy*. It
was aimed at young adolescent girls, and the moms were shocked when
they began paging through it. Its contents didn't seem appropriate for
kids that age. One article was a survey that asked the young readers if
they talked about contraception before having sex, how often they
wanted to have sex, and how often they had sex on a first date. The
mothers investigated a little closer and found articles titled "Seductive
Nights—Daring Designs That Will Make Any Night a Night to
Remember," "How to Kiss," "Swimsuits We Dare You to Wear," and
"The Truth About Boys' Bodies."

About that last article, a third mother in Wabash, Jan Dawes, had
this to say: "I've been married for 31 years. There was information in that
particular article that I found offensive and shocking. And, having had a
fulfilling relationship with my husband for 30 years, it was information
I could well have done without."[3]

But what could three mothers in Wabash, Indiana, hope to do about
a slick national magazine published in New York? The first thing they
did was to tell other mothers, who told still more. The mothers began
going to store managers and letting them know their concerns. Surprisingly, the complaints were received well, and the Hook's chain, as well as
the local Kmart, were among stores that agreed to remove the magazine.
When managers were slow to act, the mothers let them know they
wouldn't be patronizing those stores. Jan Dawes happened to be the
leader of a local Women's Aglow group in town, and it began a letter-
writing campaign to the magazine's advertisers, drawing attention to the
highly sexualized content and asking the advertisers to pull out until the
content became more suitable for the young girls it was trying to reach.

Then the mothers began contacting national media ministries,
including Concerned Women for America, broadcaster Marlin Maddox's

program, and Focus on the Family. These organizations asked their own constituencies to begin writing letters to advertisers, urging them to pull out. And one by one they did. The first to jump ship were Noxzema and Cover Girl, followed by Nair, Sea & Ski, and Tambrands. Throughout the controversy, the editor of *Sassy*, Jane Pratt, maintained that her magazine didn't intend to replace parents as the source of moral values in girls' lives. She wanted only to entertain the girls and perhaps provide them with information that could save their lives someday.

When the ad revenue started to fall, *Sassy* began softening its editorial content. But the damage was done. It couldn't recover, and it eventually went out of business, merging with *Teen*, a much more conservative magazine for girls. That mortified the *Sassy* staff. One of its editors, Christina Kelly, wrote a column in *Ms.* magazine about the whole affair, laying the blame for the magazine's demise on the letter-writing campaigns spread by Focus, Women's Aglow, and others. Kelly wrote, "You think there's freedom of the press in the USA? So did we, in our youth and naiveté. But we were wrong. Advertisers are effective censors.... If an advertiser doesn't like something, out it comes. That was it for covering sex."[4] And that was it for *Sassy*.

The Wabash mothers represent the best of Christian citizens who contribute what time and skill they have in a righteous cause. Their story reminds me of another busy Christian mom who lived a long time ago. This mother contributed her talent—writing—to the campaign against slavery in the mid 1800s. What she wrote electrified the nation and helped bring a divided country to the brink of war. Her story is told in Appendix A-2.

When the moms in Wabash began their campaign, they couldn't possibly have known where it would lead. And when Tom Wilson left his sheep farm in Vermont, he had no idea where his new path would take him. All that the mothers and the farmer knew was that they had bumped up against violations of God's moral law, and knowing the truth, they needed to respond. They were Christians. They couldn't do otherwise. That simple motivation has spurred Christians in every age to tackle injustice and evil and to give the faithful a strong—and many times controversial—heritage of social reform.

CHAPTER TWO

Christians Have Always Done Something

ONE DAY A LAWYER APPROACHED JESUS, wanting to take the measure of this popular young rabbi. The lawyer posed a question for which he already knew the answer: "What must I do to inherit eternal life?"

Sensing craftiness, Jesus turned the question back on him: "What is written in the law?"

The lawyer showed he did indeed know his Scripture: "Love the Lord your God with all your heart and with all your soul and with all your mind, and love your neighbor as yourself." Then, trying to put the spotlight back on Jesus, the man asked the question that has echoed down the ages: "And who is my neighbor?"

In response, Jesus told the story we know so well. An unfortunate traveler, making his way from Jerusalem to nearby Jericho, was set upon by thieves and left for dead, sprawled across the roadway. First a priest and then a Levite, both Jews who should have known better, passed by without helping. Then there passed by a man from Samaria, a place despised by the Jews because its inhabitants were half-breeds. If anyone had license to ignore the dying man, he did. But it was the Samaritan, the despised one, who took pity on the man, dressed his wounds, put the traveler on the Samaritan's own donkey, and helped him along to a nearby inn. In addition, the Samaritan left money to pay for the man's convalescence, and he reassured the innkeeper that he would cover whatever charges might come up.

This, said Jesus, is neighborliness, a genuine love for others that marks the person who will gain eternal life. Though the kindly act is not

17

what qualifies you or me for heaven, it does serve as evidence of the divine love within anyone who loves his neighbor because God first loved him. The story that Jesus told to the needling lawyer that day set the bar high for all who would follow Him.

The parable of the Good Samaritan defines the scope of the Christian's concern for other people—it is wide indeed. It crosses the barriers of culture, race, and creed, for if the Samaritan is neighbor to the Jew who hates him, then no one lives beyond the boundaries of our concern. We cannot wait to meet or know someone personally before acting in his or her best interests. Nor can we argue convincingly that God calls us only to care about individuals while ignoring the injustices that put so many lives, such as those of unborn children, in jeopardy. God's love stops at nothing.

If the Samaritan story defines the breadth of our compassion, it is something else that defines its depth. On the final day of creation, God brought into being the crowning achievement of His creation—man—by fashioning him in His own image. Ever since, theologians have been debating exactly what that means, but we can be sure of this much: It is our task to let others see in us a reflection of God and to realize that God's image is still evident in others, no matter how corrupt. Man was raised above all other creatures because the spark of God is in him. So we must look for that in everyone and treat people as God created them.

These twin truths, that we are neighbors to all people and that all people are of infinite worth, have made the Christian church a community marked by compassion. Down through the ages, in many different cultures, Christians have been driven by a desire to lift the sad lot of mankind wherever oppressed and ill treated. It is a divine impulse that has changed the world. To be sure, there have been periods of corruption in the organized church that have caused many to suffer, and at other times this love has been misunderstood and often rejected. But overall the impact on mankind has been tremendous. The historian Kenneth Scott Latourette has reflected on the impact of lives lived in imitation of Christ:

> No life ever lived on this planet has been so influential in the affairs of men.... From that brief life and its apparent frustration

has flowed a more powerful force for the triumphal waging of man's long battle than any other ever known by the human race.... Through it hundreds of millions have been lifted from illiteracy and ignorance, and have been placed upon the road of growing intellectual freedom and of control over their physical environment. It has done more to allay the physical ills of disease and famine than any other impulse known to man. It has emancipated millions from chattel slavery and millions of others from thralldom to vice. It has protected tens of millions from exploitation by their fellows. It has been the most fruitful source of movements to lessen the horrors of war and to put the relations of men and nations on the basis of justice and peace.[1]

REFORMISTS FROM THE BEGINNING

The church's influence began the moment the apostle Paul, responding to the Macedonian call, strode westward with the Christian message, straight into the maw of Greek culture and Roman might. The jaded philosophers on Mars Hill, who toyed with Paul as bored children torment a dog, were too smug to grasp the power of this new message. But the outcasts of Greco-Roman culture—the slaves, the half-breeds, the imprisoned, and especially the women of low and even high social class—trembled with hope in this new message and in large number embraced this God who loved them so.

Because these adherents refused to worship the old gods of Greece and Rome, the first years of Christianity were punctuated by persecution. Still, the vibrant faith spread. It outflanked one corrupt and bloodthirsty emperor after another in the first 200 years following Christ, and when three emperors in a row died horrible deaths after persecuting Christians, the next one figured that there might be a connection. In the year 313, Constantine issued an Edict of Toleration and embraced these pesky people. He grew in his appreciation of the Christian religion, although it wasn't until his deathbed that he allowed himself to be baptized. In the years of Constantine and his immediate successors, the influence of Christianity began to permeate the tottering, corrupt colossus of the empire.

Improved lives for women. In the ancient world, women were pitifully degraded, considered little better than household slaves. Now for the first time, because of the agitation of Christians, rape became a crime with severe punishment. Women obtained nearly the same right to own and control property as their husbands. Divorce laws were tightened to protect women from rejection by husband after husband, so marriage gained a status it had never held before. Adultery became a crime punishable by death. Although these reforms took centuries, the constant pressure of Christian moral belief elevated women to a status never imagined under any previous religion or political regime.

Protection for children. In ancient Rome, tyranny ruled the home. A displeased father could drag his children through the streets to the public whipping posts, keep them in chains, sell them, or murder them without any law to stop him. Unwanted infants often were simply "exposed." That is, they were abandoned by parents on the streets, only to be pounced on by human vultures and sold to witches for ritual sacrifices, or purposefully maimed and raised as beggars, or sold into slavery. In Rome, with its cult of the male warrior, it was often baby girls who met the fate of "exposure." Pressure from Christians caused Constantine and his successors to stop this vileness, although the campaign was long and hard. Finally, in 529, the emperor Justinian gave freedom to all "exposed" children who had been sold as slaves.

Shortly before the birth of Christ, a Roman businessman journeyed to Alexandria and wrote his wife who missed him. It's a tender letter in all respects except one. Here is part of the letter:

> Hilarion to Alis his wife heartiest greetings.... Know that we are still even now in Alexandria. Do not worry if when all others return I remain in Alexandria. I beg and beseech of you to take care of the little child, and, as soon as we receive wages, I will send them to you. If—good luck to you! You have a child, if it is a boy let it live; if it is a girl, throw it out. You told Aphrodisias to tell me: "Do not forget me." How can I forget you? I beg you therefore not to worry.[2]

This one bit of instruction in an otherwise loving letter jars the senses today. There is only one reason why. Christian people began to oppose such barbaric customs, often at great cost to themselves.

The lot of the slave. From the beginning of history, the prized loot of war was human chattel. Not only were captive warriors enslaved but so were civilian populations, and these wretches became the groaning engines of agriculture and commerce in any victor's domain. Against this evil, the early church fathers in the Roman world did not stand as strongly as they should have, for they regarded slavery as only one manifestation of evil in a fallen world, and one that was thoroughly entrenched. The emerging church, however, brought something new to the slave's miserable lot. Christians embraced them as people made in God's image and worthy of compassion. Gradually, as Christianity spread through the ranks of slave-owning Roman aristocrats, more and more slaves came to be set free, and those who remained enslaved often found themselves treated well. It is not hard to understand why. As one writer put it:

> It was something new when slaves went to church with their masters, and sat side by side through the service of prayers and hymns, and received together the sacrament of the Lord's Supper. Equality [prior to Christianity] came only when the slave rebelled and won his freedom at the cost of blood, when he could say to his master, "I am as good as you are." Christianity reversed all this when it induced the master to hold out his hand to the slave and say, "You are as good as I am." Slaves even entered the priesthood and heard confessions from their former masters. Justinian built a beautiful church at Ravenna, and dedicated it to the memory of a martyred slave. The old contempt and the old division lines passed when slave and master alike became one body, bond or free.[3]

Abolition of gladiatorial shows. The empire craved blood sport, and thousands of enslaved fighting men chopped and hacked at one another in Roman stadiums to amuse the emperors and their citizens. The spectacles were immense. Rome roared when the emperor Trajan unleashed 10,000 pairs of gladiators in a festival that lasted 123 days. Under Domitian, women were ordered into the stadiums to tear each other apart. In the year 391, a consul named Symmachus threw a birthday party for his young son and arranged as entertainment a fight to the death among 29 captured Saxon warriors. The prisoners became party poopers by strangling each other the night before rather than die in the arena for the amusement of Roman children.

Unbelievably, some Christians themselves, whose forebears were martyred in the Roman arenas during the years of persecution, were now to be found roaring in the stands with the pagan audiences, ignoring the admonition of their church leaders. The spectacles came to an end at the turn of the fifth century, when an eastern monk named Telemachus journeyed to the mighty city of Rome. He was determined to put a stop to the madness, armed only with faith in God and the belief that human beings made in His image should not tear each other to pieces like wild animals. Entering the Colosseum one day as a spectator, he bided his time in the stands until the fighting had raised the crowd to a frenzy. Then he leaped into the arena and separated the combatants. He was cut to pieces, but he won the day. The spectacles ceased when the emperor Honorius abolished them, moved by what had happened in the arena that day. The end of the gladiatorial contests was a significant victory for the emerging church against an entrenched pagan custom.

Humane treatment of prisoners and the poor. One of Constantine's first acts, in 315, was to bring to an end the practice of branding criminals on the forehead. He left no uncertainty about his reasons: "The human countenance, formed after the image of heavenly beauty, should not be defaced."[4] He began the practice of distributing food and clothing to poor families to keep parents from abandoning their children. In 365, Valentinian put the bishops in charge of caring for the poor, and in 529, Justinian had them take on the supervision of prisons as well, encouraging them to preach religion to the inmates. In later years, emperors contributed substantial sums to support the growing church institutions that cared for the poor, the sick, strangers, widows, and orphans.

In due course, the fondness of the emperors for the church, and the generous flow of tax money into the benevolent enterprises of the church, corrupted many of its leaders. Bishops vied for favor with the ruling elite, and aristocrats donned a thin veil of Christianity in order to be fashionable. The faith came to Rome too late to sufficiently reform it, and the emperors embraced the faith so strongly that they suffocated it. Rome fell to wave upon wave of barbarians, and as the Middle Ages broke across Europe, the church as an institution of reform fell impotent.

THE MIDDLE AGES

Here and there, embers of truth still glowed. Benedict was a monk whose cloistered order prayed seven times a day and roused themselves at midnight to sing songs of worship. Although they had separated from the world, they did so in order to preserve the good it had produced.

> The first libraries of our civilization were built by them....
> Indeed the only teachers, artists, authors of the times were
> found in the shadow of the cross. The lamp of science and lit-
> erature, burning in the cell of the monastery monk, was the
> single dim reflection of the torch of knowledge for over 500
> years.... The monks gradually moved back into the world out-
> side the monastery wall, to reclaim those whom they had once
> forsaken. In short, they began to teach: for six centuries, the
> only schools were monastery schools.[5]

Patrick was a monk sent as a missionary to Ireland. He brought them not only Christianity but also an alphabet, and he instructed the Gaelic people in its use. He started schools across northern Europe and admitted women, for the first time ever, to organized instruction. Other monks did the same: Columba brought the faith and education to Scotland, and another Celtic missionary, Columban, provoked reforms in France. The writer Frank Mead notes that modern relativists despise any education tainted by religion, yet they fail to see the broader picture—that it was the Christian church that preserved learning and brought *all* truth to people. The idea that the arts and sciences must somehow be separate from biblical teaching is a relatively new concept, one founded on ignorance of the history of education.

In this era of weakened and feuding governments, the church grew too dominant and meddled in affairs of state beyond its call. In the year 800, Pope Leo III placed a crown on the head of Charlemagne and named him the first head of the new Holy Roman Empire. For the rest of medieval history, the crown and the cross struggled for dominance. During this period, the church entered its blackest days. It pronounced its blessing on the misguided and futile Crusades, the campaigns to free the Holy Land from Muslim control. It authorized the Inquisition, the special courts that at various times used torture and killings to preserve the faithful from false teachings.

But always the church retained a reformist spirit that sought to lift man from the oppression and poverty of life. In the Middle Ages, the church possessed vast lands populated with serfs, and gradually the lot of the serf improved. The church fostered the growth of trade guilds, the forerunner of modern trade unions, in which tradesmen and artisans banded together to improve their skills and their ability to negotiate fairer circumstances for their families. In all of this, the stamp of Christianity was evident. When the work crews assembled to begin building the great cathedral of Chartres in France, their guilds required members to confess and reconcile with enemies before they could begin their work. "Such a clause might be hard to find in the agreements of modern trade unions," Mead explains. "Yet we may draw a straight line back from them to the guild worker of the Middle Ages, and on back to one who dignified and ennobled labor in a carpenter shop in Nazareth, and whose word that 'the laborer is worthy of his hire' has steadfastly lifted this man from contempt to honor in the eyes of his fellows."[6]

––––––

This, then, is a brief snapshot of the church engaged with the culture. The church flourished in the Roman persecutions, it lobbied for the oppressed when it found favor with the mighty, and it floundered when secular government officially embraced it. But in every age, its campaigns for righteousness were evident. The church tried, sometimes effectively, sometimes mistakenly, to make life better for the put-upon—the woman, the slave, and the serf.

It is difficult, however, for modern people to identify with any of this. We don't live in a world of gladiators and serfs. The Roman and medieval worlds are far removed from our day and our systems of government. Today the church is not so much at war with culture as it is at war with itself *about* culture. Should today's Christian people engage or not? Should the church stand as a bulwark athwart the quickening river of unrighteousness, or should it simply pull survivors, one by one, to a heavenly high ground and ignore the gathering flood? What happens in the church when some say yes and some say no, when believers who want to yank evil out by its roots dislodge a landslide of controversy? What does history tell us?

CHAPTER THREE

Shouldn't We Keep Away from Controversy?

IT WAS AN OCTOBER AFTERNOON IN THE YEAR 1743. John Wesley, the evangelist and reformer, worked quietly at a writing table in a friend's home in the north of England. *What was that?* he wondered. *Yelling and cursing?* The noise quickly grew to a roar. It was a mob heading directly for the house in which Wesley sat.

Then more shouts from just outside the door. "Bring out the minister! We will have the minister!" Calmly, Wesley went to the door and invited the leaders inside.

"What do you want with me?" he then inquired of the crowd, gazing at them directly, his voice calm, his manner pleasant.

"We want you to go with us to the justice," they said.

"That I will, with all my heart," Wesley replied gently.[1]

The mob, several hundred strong, marched Wesley for two miles, through the gathering gloom and a chilly rain, to the magistrate's house in Wednesbury, only to find that he wouldn't be disturbed. On to neighboring Walsall and another magistrate. But neither would he arrest Wesley.

Curious, this. The Anglican vicar of Wednesbury had been railing against these "Methodists," as they were derisively called, these ridiculous enthusiasts who were trying to reform the decayed institutions of British society and in so doing were upsetting the settled church life of good people all over England. Responding to the vicar, local magistrates had ordered the arrest of any Methodist preacher spotted in the area. Now they had not just any Methodist preacher but the head man himself, and they didn't seem to want him.

Confused, and with their numbers dwindling in the downpour, the mob headed Wesley back to Wednesbury. They hadn't gone a hundred yards when they met another mob, also looking for Wesley. Full of fresh fury, this Walsall gang quickly overpowered the first bunch and then started in on Wesley. One brute rushed for him and swung a heavy club several times. If only one of the blows had landed, as Wesley later recalled, "it would have saved all further trouble."[2] Someone hit him in the chest. He was punched in the mouth, and blood flowed. Somehow he spotted a half-open door and groped toward it.

It was the mayor's house, but the mayor pushed him back out, fearing the mob would tear down the house if Wesley were allowed in. On the doorstep, Wesley turned to the throng and asked if they would listen to him. They cried out: "No! No! Knock his brains out! Down with him! Kill him at once!" Others wanted to hear him, and he spoke a while until his voice faltered. The shouting began again and Wesley started praying aloud.

Inexplicably, the thug leading the mob, a burly prizefighter, suddenly changed his mind and decided to protect Wesley. Others joined him, and a fistfight broke out among the rioters, but Wesley's newfound protectors got him safely away. Amazed by the incident, Wesley attributed the mob leader's sudden change of heart to God's intervention.

REVIVAL NATURALLY LEADS TO REFORM

Physical assaults, some of them occurring even while he was in the pulpit, were common for John Wesley. Two mobs at the same time, however, was novel. These were the early years of the Wesleyan revival in England, a mighty evangelical reform movement known as "Methodism" because of its then-peculiar style of intense prayer, worship, and Christian reformist activity. Wesley converted thousands in huge, open-air revival meetings. The settings for his rallies were an affront to the religious establishment, but he had no choice. The pulpits of the sedate, establishment Anglican churches were closed to him, and the existing church buildings couldn't begin to hold his growing crowds anyway.

Wesley offended many church and political leaders of his day

because he came to believe that "good works are the inseparable proper-
ties of living faith, even as warmth and light are the inseparable proper-
ties of the sun."[3] Two Wesleyan maxims, indelibly imprinted upon his
followers, were these:

1. "The gospel of Christ knows of no religion but social, no
   holiness but social holiness."
2. "I look upon all the world as my parish."[4]

The problems he and his Christian reformers took on were immense:
the forced labor of children, indentured servitude, slavery, rampant drunkenness, the poor health of the peasant class, prison abuse, and lack of education for the exploited poor. A contemporary French writer distilled the
essence of the Wesleyan reforms by touching at the heart of his movement—man's love for his fellow man in imitation of God's love for man.
The writer said of Wesley and his reformers: "They appeal always and
everywhere from the miserable reality to the human conscience. They
make one see the man in the criminal, the brother in the negro. They
introduced a new personage into the social and political world of Aristo-
cratic England—the fellow man. [And that fellow man] never more will
leave the stage."[5]

It would be difficult to exaggerate Wesley's impact. Some historians
speculate that if there had been an American Wesley, slavery might have
dissipated in the United States without a civil war, just as it did in England. There, the great evangelical movement that grew from Wesley's
preaching set the stage for another evangelical, William Wilberforce, to
lead a frustrating but peaceable and ultimately successful 20-year campaign in Parliament to abolish the slave trade in the British colonies in
1833. (We'll come back to Wilberforce in chapter 10.)

HARSH CRITICISMS

From the safe distance of so many years, it is easy for Christians today to
bask in the glow of the accomplishments of a John Wesley. Were he on

the scene today, however, many Christians wouldn't be so sure that he was a worthy role model. In standing for righteousness he attracted severe and unrelenting critics.

In 1750, 12 years after Wesley's conversion and after the revivals had begun under his preaching, an Anglican churchman, John Kirkby, wrote about "the horrid blasphemies and impieties taught by those diabolical seducers called Methodists. They pray in the language of a saint to Beelzebub himself.... Their religion could be forged nowhere else but in the bottomless pit.... [John Wesley is] that emissary of Satan [whose religion is] as opposite to Christianity as heaven is to hell [and whose] damnation will be just."[6] A history of England, also published in 1750, described Wesley's influence this way: "Imposture and fanaticism will hang upon the skirts of religion. Weak minds were seduced by the delusions of a superstition, styled Methodism, raised upon affectation of superior sanctity and pretension to divine illumination."[7]

The onslaught did not soon abate. In 1808 the *Edinburgh Review* carried an editorial that said, "We shall use the general term of Methodism to designate those ... classes of fanatics, not troubling ourselves to point out the finer shades and nicer discriminations of lunacy, but treating them all as in one general conspiracy against common sense and rational, orthodox, Christianity."[8]

The elite members of British society, the "Hollywood crowd" of Wesley's day, were especially nasty. A historian of the period notes:

Priests, bishops, historians, journalists, magistrates and squires by no means monopolized this aggressive opposition. Sir Robert Walpole the politician, Pope the poet, Fielding the novelist, Lord Northington the judge, Butler the theologian, Foote the dramatist, Hume the philosopher, Hogarth the painter, Lady Buckingham the smart society leader, Horace Walpole the literary man about town, and Cobbett the demagogue—these are but a few of the notabilities who enlisted in the solemn campaign to exorcise the hated specter of "Methodism," which was haunting the arctic specter of English life.[9]

Wesley was deterred by none of this. He expected to be attacked for his assault on sin, for it fastened like barnacles to the foundations of society's institutions, corrupting them and weakening them, and sin must be rooted out and plucked off. Who better to take on these tasks than Christian converts? Wesley understood that salvation is not the end of the story for those who come to Christ. Rather, it is the beginning of a life lived in service to God's sacred creation, mankind. And if that life of service attracts controversy and opposition, well, what could be more normal?

WILLIAM BOOTH FINDS HIS CALLING

England did not succumb permanently to Wesley's campaign for righteousness. A century after him, the nation was chugging and belching its way through an Industrial Revolution on the path to modernity, spewing human refuse in its wake. By 1865, London, a city of 3 million, had 100,000 citizens in poverty and thousands more teetering on the brink of it. The lower classes were easily exploited by the rich and the influential, and the Wesleyan fire was sputtering.

One night, a lanky, stoop-shouldered man strode through the streets of the hellish East London slum, stricken by what he saw:

> He thrust past hulking laborers and women clad only in soiled petticoats. Children with wolfish faces foraged at his feet, gobbling up heaps of decaying plums in the street market's garish light.... He saw five-year-olds blind drunk at tap-room doorways; mothers forcing beer from white-chipped jugs down babies' throats. Outside pub after pub silent savage men with ashen faces, coats piled nearby, lunged and struck and toppled heavily.... Beyond the intense white glare of naphtha men passed furtively, blood-soaked handkerchiefs cloaking the shivering bodies of dogs that had lost a fight.... The whole city stank. Even the Thames. Almost 370 sewers flushed into its yellow-grey water. Between Westminster and London bridge, a

sticky black bank of sewage, six feet deep, stretched 100 feet into the main channel, creating a stench so appalling that in summer no member of Parliament could use the House of Commons library.[10]

William Booth wasn't repulsed by the sights that assailed him. Far from it. He only grew more excited as he walked, and he quickened his pace. When he finally reached his rickety little apartment, he swept his wife, Catherine, into his arms, his eyes burning with intensity. He told her that the downtrodden of London were to be his life's work.

It was a blind leap into the lap of God. For 13 years this Methodist circuit-riding preacher, who had never quite found his stride, had been skirting poverty himself, and now he and Catherine had six small children. His decision to break from his tiny, diffident Methodist congregations and launch himself at the plight of the poor would surely sink him.

Night after night, Booth dragged home late, exhausted after his preaching missions on the city's streets. He called drunks from their stupors and prostitutes from their tawdry parlors, offering salvation in Jesus Christ as the only exit from the hellish lock of sin. Many times he returned to Catherine in tattered and bloodied clothes, for not every ruffian welcomed the news of salvation.

RECRUITING AN ARMY

Booth's ranks of converts grew slowly. He eventually recruited assistants, mostly converts from the streets, and they began to think of themselves as soldiers in perennial attack against the devil. They proclaimed themselves enlisted for the duration, and they wielded conversion to Christ as their only weapon. They were an army, a Salvation Army, as Booth declared suddenly at a meeting in 1878—a bit presumptuous, perhaps, since at the time his "army" had a mere 88 members.

Booth was barred from respectable Methodist churches because his converts stank them up, and they felt ill at ease anyway. So he rented dance halls and saloons for his evangelistic meetings. Not only were these surroundings familiar to his seekers but so were the worship songs. Salvationists fitted out familiar drinking ditties with sacred lyrics: "Champagne Charley Is My Name" became "Bless His Name, He Sets Me Free," and "Good Old Whiskey" was refurbished as "Storm the Forts of Darkness."[11] In another insult to decorous Christianity, brass bands began marching through the red-light districts to call the drunks' attention to Booth's evangelistic rallies.

Among the saved were hundreds of young prostitutes who told shocking tales of being enticed into London from the hinterlands, raped, and—thus shamed from ever returning home—forced into prostitution. Procurement rings were large and well organized. Upstanding businessmen, professionals, and even members of Parliament paid handsomely to bed down virgins in the city's many brothels. There were 80,000 prostitutes in the city and 2,000 pimps alone in the square mile around the Charing Cross section of the city.

Booth and his lieutenants waded in. They sent a young Salvationist lass to penetrate the prostitution trade, and she poured forth fact after fact to a courageous newspaper editor. The articles shocked the city and forced Parliament to act by introducing a bill raising the age of sexual consent for women to 16. When powerful men sought to divert the bill, Booth organized a massive petition drive and delivered an unheard-of 393,000 signatures to Parliament on a scroll two and a half miles long. The bill passed.

This wasn't the Army's only foray into public policy. England's recession of 1887 threw thousands out of work, often in brutal fashion. A workingman's first gray hair got him booted for being too old, and rheumatism, cataracts, and similar diseases cost people their jobs as well. Trade unions were limited. Unemployment compensation, health benefits, and pensions were all unknown. Thousands of men huddled on benches and around campfires in London parks, slowly starving.

Things worsened when 10,000 dockworkers struck in 1889, but the Army quickly moved in with 195,000 cheap meals. Booth began the nation's first labor exchange, in seven years' time placing 69,000 men in jobs. Labor yards opened at each Army shelter. He also started a missing person's bureau to locate some of the 9,000 a year who dropped from sight in London. He sought housing and legal aid for the poor, as well as

a bank for them, all the while critiquing England's laissez-faire governmental policies that neglected the poor.

CRUEL OPPOSITION

Booth's critique earned him a scathing rebuttal from Thomas Huxley, the
esteemed professor who popularized Darwin's theories on the survival of the
fittest. Booth's campaigns for the poor were only a scheme to drive shorn
sheep into his "narrow theological fold." The undying allegiance of Salvationist officers to Booth was, for Huxley, a worse evil than drunkenness or
prostitution. In 12 letters to the editor of the *Times* of London, he cut Booth
to ribbons. Other enemies began to weigh in. Various publications called
him a sensual, dishonest, sanctimonious, and hypocritical scoundrel; a
brazen-faced charlatan; a pious rogue; a masquerading hypocrite; and Field
Marshal von Booth.[12] Angered by the attacks, Booth's son Bramwell was also
frustrated that his father wouldn't respond to them. Booth said, "Bramwell,
fifty years hence it will matter very little indeed how these people treated us.
It will matter a great deal how we dealt with the work of God."[13]

As the years rolled by and the ranks of the saved grew, the Army's frontal
attack on sin began carving deep lines into Satan's territory. Too many bar and
brothel habitués were becoming Christians, and some of these developed into
fervent Salvationist preachers who were especially effective in reaching their
former bar-stool brethren. Fearing a loss of business, brothel and tavern owners began to fight back. "The Army learned the bleak truth of the Spanish
proverb: 'He who would be a Christ must expect crucifixion.' "[14]

One night at a dockside rally, drunken seamen fired their ship's guns
at close range toward a group of Salvationist ladies. Miraculously, no one
was killed. Elsewhere, another squad of Army lasses were bound with
ropes and assaulted with live coals. Still others were ambushed by ruffians throwing hot tar and burning sulfur. A recruit was beaten so savagely
that he lay in a coma for three days.

Many men who should have known better whipped the mobs
to greater frenzy. At Hastings, the town's leading grocer offered
rotten eggs to all comers as anti-Salvation ammunition. At

Folkstone, Kent, a clergyman sent a public message to the Army Captain: "Is the peace of this town to be disturbed night after night for a bastard flag that represents nothing and nobody?" And he went further: a cash prize would go to the first tough capturing the Army's banner and bearing it to his study. Promptly Mayor Edwin Bradman added fuel to the flame: "Drive them all into the harbor or into hell. Take their flags and tie them around their necks and hang 'em." From then on Folkestone Salvationists ran a merciless gauntlet of hooting fishermen. Roads were blocked against them with the masts of fishing [boats]; fish refuse and rocks burst about them.

No General to hang back,... Booth was often in the thick of it. When a curbside rough spat at him on a Midlands tour, Booth curbed a solicitous aide: "Don't rub it off—it's a medal." At Sheffield, in January, 1882, his generalship was tested to the full: a monster procession ... tramped steadily... towards the city's Albert Hall. Ahead rattled a wagonette with a brass band playing lustily.... In the rearguard, scores of uniformed Salvationists kept step behind the General's carriage. A sidelong glance showed close on 1,000 cloth-capped ruffians, called "The Sheffield Blades," ... jeering and gibing. Suddenly, with a blood-curdling yell, they spilled into the roadway, streaking like furies for the Army's line of march.

Flying clods of soft wet mud hailed about the band; mud choked and blinded them and the music wavered. A stone struck Lt. Davidson clean between the eyes; as he swayed in the saddle, half blind with pain, a flying cudgel caught him an agonizing welt across the base of his skull. Somehow [fellow officers drove off his attackers], propping Davidson on his mount until the hall was reached. "I hope they'll get saved," [Davidson] whispered, then the world went dark. Removed to a hospital, he lay concussed for weeks upon the brink of death.

Through it all, Booth stood bolt upright in his carriage, mud and dead cats hurtling past him, his face a graven mask as he barked crisp orders.... They heard his rallying cry, his arms outstretched to receive cornets and tubas that hard-pressed bandsmen were thrusting at him. At length, when all had reached the Albert Hall, his battered, bleeding cohorts were ordered direct to the platform. At the sight of their buckled instruments, the uniforms smeared with blood and egg yolk, a low buzz of horror stirred the vast audience, rising to an angry clamor of protest. "Now's the time to get your photographs taken," Booth told his aides with grim humor.[15]

Nor did the Salvationists escape persecution beyond England's borders. Although Booth sent his capable daughter Kate personally to lead the campaign in Switzerland, the Salvationists suffered bitterly in Geneva, the center of John Calvin's theology of election. That doctrine says that those who are destined for heaven have been predetermined by God, and no one can turn to Christ without God's help. To Genevans, the Army's open invitations sounded bizarre. Vicious brawling broke out at the third meeting in Geneva, and although Kate appealed for police protection, it did not come. In one village outside Geneva, Salvationists were fined when their joyful songs drowned out the drunken tones of an alcoholic who was also trying to sing.

Eventually it became illegal to wear Army uniforms in public, and Kate was soon expelled from the city, went to Bern, and fought against the legal proscriptions from there. She failed. Although Army services continued without uniforms, rocks and bottles and fistfights were a steady feature of Army worship in Switzerland, as the magistrates in canton after canton resisted the effective evangelism of the Salvationists. Economic boycotts against them began, and they could not buy food or clothing anywhere. Still, they wouldn't cease, and after protracted courtroom appearances, they finally regained the right to wear their uniforms in public. Immediately, Salvation-style bonnets for the ladies and navy blue in general became anathema in Swiss fashion circles.

The Army Flourishes Anyway

Despite all the opposition, the work of the Salvation Army continued to grow worldwide. By 1883, the Army was renting more than 400 buildings that seated half a million people for services. Often these were dank, drafty, and smelly—slaughterhouses, a brewery yard, bars, sawmills, and warehouses. Money was so short that food for the troops, not the violent opposition, was actually Booth's chief concern. In 1878, he had to issue a "General Order Against Starvation" as a warning to his officers to take better care of themselves. One of them, Officer Mary Jane Casley, often fainted from hunger as she preached. In Napa City, California, several officers who were pelted with onions and stale rolls happily collected all of it as manna from heaven. Elsewhere, a recruit learned the art of buttering bread with a paintbrush instead of a knife.

The numbers being reached by the famished Army were astonishing. One survey taken in London showed that, in 1882, 17,000 were worshiping in Army facilities, compared to 11,000 in ordinary churches. All told, between 1881 and 1885, some 250,000 people made decisions for Christ as a result of the Army's ministry. By 1890 they were operating 2,900 centers and preaching 50,000 times a week. The Army's publication, the *War Cry*, was reaching 31 million in various editions. By the time Booth died in 1912, after 60 years as an evangelist and despite the incredible viciousness of the attacks against him, Booth had become a national hero in England. Some 150,000 people filed past his casket in three days, and 40,000 attended his funeral service, including one woman sitting unobtrusively toward the back, England's Queen Mary, long a Booth admirer. Over the years, Booth had recruited 16,000 officers who worked in 58 countries and 34 languages.

In 1958 a Swiss postal official was trying to decide on new designs for the country's stamps. By that time, the persistent Salvation Army had finally secured a foothold in Switzerland and had grown to 400 officers and 120 local organizations working in 22 Swiss cantons. The Army had become well accepted into Swiss life. One of the Swiss postage stamp designs chosen that year was a navy blue Salvation Army bonnet, in honor of the Army's upcoming 75th anniversary.

Wesley's Methodism and Booth's Salvation Army are household names today, while safely forgotten are the brutal reprisals—often from fellow churchmen—against these courageous founders. Had they quailed in the face of physical danger on the streets and from ridicule in high places, they never would have accomplished their far-reaching results. By their persistent good works, they turned many skeptics into ardent supporters, and as for the entrenched critics, they were either simply outlasted or ignored, because Wesley and Booth clung only to God and to the righteousness of their cause.

Part Two

There's More to Christianity than Saving Souls

CHAPTER FOUR

Why It's Right to Do What's Right

IF WE LEARN ANYTHING FROM PEOPLE LIKE John Wesley and William Booth, it is that these men had deep concern for the lost souls of the unredeemed. More than anything else they wanted to see people saved. This is evangelism, the central mission of the church. But to these men, evangelism was not the last step. They saw beyond the Christian conversion of an unsaved person to the plight he was in, and they were not content to ignore those circumstances, even though such convictions brought them turmoil, controversy, hatred, and at times physical danger.

Why not simply bring a person to salvation and let it go at that, since the convert's future is secure for all eternity? One avoids much controversy, and the church escapes charges of "politics" and partisanship. But it isn't as simple as that. I saw this firsthand when I visited the Central American nation of Nicaragua. Perhaps it was a strange place to learn a lesson about the American church and social issues, but it is a lesson I've never forgotten.

For most of the twentieth century, Nicaragua was led by puppet governments riddled with corruption, the result of the viselike grip of the ruling Somoza family, first the father and then the son. Over the years, the Somoza oligarchy had grown fat. It had gained control of the Nicaraguan national airline, the steamship line, two-thirds of the fishing industry, half of the sugar mills, and one-third of all the tillable land in the country.

Yet the populace was neglected. By the 1970s, the infant mortality rate was nine times that of the United States. Eighty percent of all Nicaraguans had no running water, and there were 20,000 cases of advanced tuberculosis.

Life expectancy was about 50 years; the illiteracy rate stood at 50 percent; and only 1 in 20 Nicaraguans finished elementary school. Throughout these years, it is sad to say, Nicaragua under the Somozas was dominated by the United States, so much so that the American ambassador's face appeared with Somoza's on the Nicaraguan 20-cordoba bill.

On top of all that, disaster struck. Two days before Christmas in 1972, a half hour after midnight, the capital city of Managua shuddered under a massive earthquake and crumpled. Nearly 10,000 people died, and a quarter of a million were instantly homeless. The city was prostrate. Other countries rushed in to help, but all the financial aid flowed through the agencies of the Somoza family. A year later, after nearly $200 million in foreign aid had been sent, the capital city was still in rubble, its people badly cared for. Some of the money was sponged up by Somoza's construction companies, and some of it purchased rebuilding sites from Somoza's friends and family at bloated prices.

Because of this injustice, rage rose and rose until it burst in rivers of blood. The protracted Nicaraguan Civil War in the 1970s, between Somoza's army and the leftist Sandinista guerrillas, was so ferocious that by the summer of 1979, when Somoza fled for his life to Miami, 50,000 people had died—five times the number killed by the earthquake.

That earthquake and the revolution not only destroyed Nicaragua's capital city and its economy but they also demolished complacency in the hearts of the country's evangelical pastors. For the first time, these church leaders began working together on something more than evangelism. Evangelical pastors in the city organized 1,100 volunteers, who cooked 30,000 hot breakfasts in the days following the calamity of the earthquake. The pastors surprised themselves about what they could accomplish working together. This was the beginning of CEPAD—the Evangelical Committee for Aid and Development—a nationwide alliance of Protestant churches.

AFTERSHOCKS

In 1974, two years after the earthquake and still five years away from the bloody coup of 1979, some 300 Protestant pastors gathered at a retreat to reflect on what they had accomplished together after the earthquake and on what their Christianity should mean to them in the black days ahead. They also tried to consider whether they should have done more to stand up to the governmental corruption before things had a chance to get so bad. Yes, they decided at the retreat, they should have done more.

During their meditation together, pastor after pastor swallowed hard on the parable of the Good Samaritan. Deep within themselves, the pastors recognized that the young Sandinista revolutionaries, full of misplaced Marxist zeal, had been surpassing the Christians—supposedly the spiritual heirs of the Good Samaritan—in standing up to Somoza's injustice on behalf of the hurting people of Nicaragua. These evangelical pastors could never become revolutionaries themselves, as had some of the Catholic priests who had actually taken to the hills. But evangelicals should never have ignored the governmental injustice.

One of the ministers who went on that retreat in 1974 was Rodolfo Fonseca, a Church of God pastor in Managua, who reflected back on that experience for me during a trip I made to Nicaragua to try sorting all of this out.[1] He said:

> As Christians, we were surrounded by wounded people, injured people. It is not revolution that should teach us social responsibility; it is the Bible. How could we Christians be preaching only the spiritual part and let the so-called Marxist atheists do what we were supposed to be doing? It was that kind of Christianity [emphasizing only spiritual matters] that our missionaries with blond hair and blue eyes and the fragrance of heaven taught us. If we preach only the spiritual side, then the revolutionaries are showing themselves to be more Christian than are we who claim to be Christian.

At that point another pastor, Nicanor Mairena, joined the discussion:

> I was educated under the control of the North Americans. They prohibited us from politics. I accepted that. But after three

years of the revolution, I have become convinced of the opposite. North Americans don't suffer lack. Your main necessity is
that of the soul, and your [church] culture was transmitted to
us. In the first place, it is necessary for the soul to be saved. In
the second place, it is necessary for the body to be saved—from
illness, from malnutrition, from illiteracy. How can someone
serve the Lord well if he is undernourished?

Not all the evangelical pastors thought like Nicanor did during those
years. Many of them, perhaps even the majority, continued to stay out of
"politics" and concentrated on the gospel of salvation. But some of them,
especially the younger ones, came to believe that the gospel of Jesus
Christ had a dimension not taught by the American missionaries. It was
a dimension of earthly justice for this life, not just heavenly salvation for
the next. They learned about it not from books or from teachers but
from the rugged experience of an earthquake and a revolution.

There is an epilogue to this story. To the people of Nicaragua, the
Sandinista Marxists were ultimately unpopular. Responding to international pressure, they held democratic elections, and the people, nervous
about the Sandinistas' growing alignment with Cuba, eventually threw
them out.

DOING THE RIGHT THING

Should the pastors have been willing to stand against their corrupt government? Were they right to ignore politics while the suffering of their
people became intolerable? They themselves came to believe that they
should have done more, and they were convicted by the parable of the
Good Samaritan.

Our country, of course, is not pressed under a dictator's thumb, but
we are no less burdened. Goodness is slowly being pushed out of the
American way. We have no justification for being complacent. In the face
of our society's growing evil, what is the role of Christian people? What
in the world would Jesus do?

Well, Jesus would do what He spoke of in His famous talk so many years ago. Jesus, in the Sermon on the Mount, offered encouragement to those who care deeply not only about salvation in the next life but also about righteousness in this one.

Righteousness—doing the right thing, whether it is something that must be acted upon or something that must be believed or something that must be stood for—is a towering theme in the Bible, and the hearts of the Nicaraguan pastors were rightly seared by it. Doing what is right is something that all of us should take to heart, particularly because we are living in a society whose moral underpinnings are being eroded by people who are so ready to do the wrong thing.

In the Sermon on the Mount, Jesus delivered eight beatitudes, or profound "declarations of blessing," upon people who take His words seriously and try to put them into practice. Among those beatitudes, Jesus mentioned one of the blessed traits not once but twice. That trait is righteousness. Jesus said, "Blessed are those who hunger and thirst for righteousness, for they will be filled" (Matthew 5:6). And again, four verses later, He said, "Blessed are those who are persecuted because of righteousness, for theirs is the kingdom of heaven" (Matthew 5:10).

What is this thing called *righteousness*—a term Jesus twice elevated to a level of profound significance in that list of eight beatitudes?

THE MEANING OF RIGHTEOUSNESS

Righteousness is a broad term, as Jesus used it. Simply put, righteousness means what is right or just, as measured by God, and God's standard of measure is perfection. The most important meaning of righteousness for us as human beings centers on the fact that we cannot measure up to God's standard, so we deserve to be separated from Him forever in hell. The profound good news is that God has taken care of this problem, according to the apostle Paul in his letter to the Romans, by imputing (attributing, or reckoning to our account) righteousness to us as a gift, through Christ, who paid the penalty for our sins by His death on the cross.

But righteousness means more than that. In the Hebrew culture, people thought far more about the community than they did about the individual. Righteousness was not primarily about one person's relationship with God; it was the standard for right relationships between people.

The Hebrew word for *righteousness* is also translated as *justice*. And God cares a great deal about it. Through the prophet Amos, He declared, "Let justice roll on like a river, righteousness like a never-failing stream!" (Amos 5:24).

Certainly this passion for a righteous society was part of Jesus' meaning when He pronounced His blessing on those who hunger and thirst to see righteousness dominate the affairs of mankind. The Revised English Bible translates Matthew 5:6 this way: "Blessed are those who hunger and thirst to see right prevail; they shall be satisfied."

This explains, of course, why Jesus had something to say about those who are "persecuted because of righteousness" (verse 10). Many of the prophets ran into trouble when they stood up for righteousness in a society that had rebelled against it.

This corporate aspect of righteousness is not stressed nearly as often today as the Pauline one, and there is ample explanation for this. In the latter years of the nineteenth century, as a result of new thinking about the Bible that emanated from Europe, some segments of mainline American Christianity began losing faith in the Bible as God's infallible Word. They lost faith in the resurrection of Christ and the reality of eternal life in heaven, among other things. So what was left of Christianity? Only its outward shell—the doing of good works, the betterment of society through social projects designed to uplift the downtrodden. This came to be known as the Social Gospel movement.

Concerned about this erosion of orthodox Christian belief, a broad group of distinguished conservative theologians joined hands from 1909 to 1912 to publish a series of 12 booklets emphasizing the fundamentals of the faith. They included such doctrines as Christ's incarnation, His atonement for sins by His death on the cross, His literal resurrection from the dead, His Second Coming, and the realities of heaven and hell. The booklets were titled *The Fundamentals,* and their publication began what was to become known as the fundamentalist movement within the Christian church. Fundamentalists emphasized the salvation of lost souls rather than the social concerns of the downtrodden—concerns that characterized their opponents.

WHAT COULD MATCH EVANGELISM?

How does social action stack up today against evangelism? Isn't evangelism the point of evangelical Christianity? Isn't it much more important than attending to the temporal needs of our neighbor? Doesn't a person's welfare for all eternity supersede his need for food, or his need for transportation, or his need for an honest, responsive government? Of course it does. But if you place this question before the Protestant pastors of Nicaragua, they will tell you that by attending to the temporal needs of people, you honor the God of love. Moreover, you win a hearing for people's eternal needs.

Even so, where is the limit? Everyone understands that it is a good thing to bind up a traveler's wounds and take him to an inn, or to fetch gas for a mother stranded in her car. These actions aren't controversial. But what about those that are? Shouldn't we avoid offending people?

The real question we should be asking is this: What does righteousness command? In other words, what is the right thing to do? The abortion battle is controversial and political, but does that make it right to stand idly by while unborn children are killed? The battle to define the family is controversial today, but does that make it any less right and proper that a child should be raised by both a mother and a father? Or that people should avoid having sex until they can provide a child with a loving, stable home cemented by their own committed marital relationship?

In his first epistle, John puts this very directly: "Dear children, do not let anyone lead you astray. He who does what is right is righteous, just as he [Christ] is righteous" (1 John 3:7). John also explains that doing righteous deeds will sometimes bring the hatred of the world as the only response: "Do not be like Cain, who belonged to the evil one and murdered his brother. And why did he murder him? Because his own actions were evil and his brother's were righteous. Do not be surprised, my brothers, if the world hates you" (1 John 3:12-13). Some deeds of righteousness bring the world's admiration and others bring the world's condemnation. But what is right is right.

Many times, Christians are afraid to stand boldly for righteousness, particularly in public, because they fear being controversial and because people who need to hear the gospel might be repelled from the church or from friendships with Christians. John is telling us, in effect, not to worry about that but instead to stand for righteousness and to expect a certain amount of hostility. After all, no one can convict a sinner about his need for salvation; that is up to the Holy Spirit. When a leader ducks the cause of righteousness in an attempt to retain the good graces of unsaved people, he is usurping the Spirit's role.

In 1982, a conference of conservative evangelical missionary leaders convened in Grand Rapids, Michigan, to grapple with these issues. They sought to bring into balance the activities of social action and evangelism. They concluded in their report that these two arenas of ministry are integral to one another. The report said that they are "like the two blades of a pair of scissors or the two wings of a bird."[2]

The leaders delineated three ways in which social responsibility and evangelism dovetail with each other:

> First, social responsibility is a consequence of evangelism. That is, our salvation should result in social responsibility. Paul wrote in Galatians 5:6 that "faith works through love." James says, "I will show you my faith through my works." Titus 2:14 tells us that Christ came not only to "redeem us from all wickedness," but also "to purify for himself a people that are his very own, eager to do what is good." Similarly, Ephesians 2:10 teaches that Christians are "created in Christ Jesus to do good works, which God prepared in advance for us to do." [Thus, the writers of the Grand Rapids report noted that] good works cannot save, but they are an indispensable evidence of salvation.... Social responsibility, like evangelism, should therefore be included in the teaching ministry of the church.

Secondly, social activity can be a bridge to evangelism. It can break down prejudice and suspicion, open closed doors, and gain a hearing for the gospel.... If we turn a blind eye to the suffering, the social oppression, the alienation and loneliness of people, let us not be surprised if they turn a deaf ear to our message of eternal salvation.

Thirdly, social activity not only follows evangelism as its consequence and aim, and precedes it as a bridge, but also accompanies it as its partner. In His own ministry, Jesus went about teaching and preaching, and also doing good and healing. Both were expressions of His compassion for people, and both should be of ours.... Thus evangelism and social responsibility, while distinct from one another, are integrally related in our proclamation of and obedience to the Gospel. The partnership is, in reality, a marriage.[3]

The conference delegates recognized that sometimes Christian acts of compassion will be controversial. They distinguished between activities that are appreciated by most people and activities that often are unwelcome to a particular faction. As they saw it, the two groups are as follows:

Social Service	Social Action
Relieving human need	Removing the causes of human need
Philanthropic activity	Political/economic activity
Ministering to individuals and families	Transforming the structures of society
Works of mercy	The quest for justice[4]

Social action comprises those activities that are usually scoffed at by some Christian leaders as "political" and therefore inappropriate for Christians' participation. But think about it for a moment. In his effort to end the suffering of slaves in America, the abolitionist Theodore Weld might have hewn literally to the parable of the Good Samaritan and limited his campaign against slavery to binding the individual wounds of beaten slaves, seeing that they were cared for until they healed, only to be returned to the fields and mistreated again. When evil is rampant, as it was with slavery, an individual work of mercy is almost futile because the need is too great. The quest for justice becomes imperative. (Read Weld's exciting story in Appendix A-1.)

SOCIAL ACTION DOESN'T BLOCK EVANGELISM

Sometimes those very Christian leaders who take on the issues of righteousness prove to be very successful at evangelism. Jerry Falwell is often used as an example of a man who has brought unhelpful controversy to the cause of Christ because of his public campaigns for righteousness. Falwell points out, however, that he pastors a church of 22,000 members, most of whom were led to Christ during the time when his organization, Moral Majority, was staking out some highly controversial positions.

Similarly, the reach of Focus on the Family continues to grow. Some Christian leaders are critical of Dr. James Dobson for wading into issues that attract unfriendly press coverage, fearing that the controversies will drive people from the gospel. But in fact, many people are brought to the Lord by Dr. Dobson's programs, which regularly offer a salvation message. There is no necessary conflict between motivating people to become Christians and motivating Christians to let their voices be heard when issues of righteousness are at stake.

Each year at its annual meeting, the Southern Baptist Convention adopts strong, politically incorrect, and controversial (in the world's eyes) resolutions on a variety of current social issues. Yet the Southern Baptist Convention remains the country's largest Protestant denomination and is growing fast. That growth has come because of evangelism, and the evangelism works in tandem with the Southern Baptists' strongly held and publicly recorded beliefs on issues of righteousness.

The greatest evangelist of the twentieth century was certainly not concerned that evangelism would suffer if Christian people took up bold positions on issues of moral righteousness. In an article he wrote some time ago, Billy Graham called Christians to account for failing to stand against injustices: "Our motto too often seems to be, 'Stay aloof. Don't get involved. Let somebody else stick his neck out.' In the face of all kinds of conditions screaming to be rectified, too many of us find ourselves afflicted with moral laryngitis."[5] In this short article, Graham moved fluidly between the basics of Christian faith and the moral causes that emanate from faith. He wrote:

> Christianity grew because its adherents were not silent. They said, "We cannot but speak the things we have seen and heard [a reference to the message of evangelism]." Nor did they stop with expressing the great faith they had found. They stormed against the evils of their day until the very foundations of decadent Rome began to crumble. Is the church doing that today?[6]

Graham cited several results of those who take stands for righteousness. First, moral courage "floods the spirit with vitality," and he gave as an example a group of high school students who took a successful stand against a porno movie theater. Second, courage is contagious, and he wrote about an incident in which one student stood against racial discrimination in his fraternity. That student's courage infected others in the fraternity, and finally there was a change in the way racial minorities were treated. Finally, Graham wrote that great men grow from commitment to great causes, and among his examples was Peter, who once cringed before a servant girl who identified him as a follower of Christ. It was the same Peter, Graham observed, who later became a great evangelist, one of those who "turned the world upside down" for Christ.

Graham himself was never known as a social reformer, and throughout his career he stuck close to his calling as a mass crusade evangelist. But this appeal to the general church, published in a popular magazine of immense circulation, came in the midst of social fury over civil rights in the South. Although the evangelical church by and large sat out that great cause, Graham's message lent credence to the evangelical battles against abortion, pornography, and feminism that were to arise in the 1970s.

It is true that when some Christian people speak out on a controversial issue, they repel others from the gospel. All of us have winced occasionally at the harsh tone and condemning spirit of some in whom the love of Christ is plainly absent. It is not so much what we say as Christians but how we say it that is important. For years, in my public policy role at Focus on the Family, I have given speeches and presentations and have been a participant in panel discussions in a multitude of secular, hostile environments. Many times these have provided wonderful opportunities for explaining not only the position at hand but also what lies behind it—that is, the Christian faith from which our moral standard flows. I found that one's demeanor in such situations often determines the secularists' response. (There is much more to be said about this in chapter 10.)

As evangelical Christians, we inherit a tradition that has preserved the Bible as the authoritative Word of God in the face of concerted attacks. For that we can all be grateful. But at the same time, our heritage has often given too little heed to the full breadth of Christ's command to be salt and light in the world. That is why the work of the thinkers in Grand Rapids was so important, and it is why some Nicaraguan pastors discovered the need for a different dimension to church work in their troubled country, one they hadn't learned from their American missionary teachers.

But what does this mean for the local church here at home?

CHAPTER FIVE

Churches and Caesar

NO PASTOR WANTS HIS CHURCH TO BECOME "politicized," but merely by addressing some of the more controversial social issues from the pulpit, he will run that risk. Nonetheless he must step up to the task, because in our day secular government has stepped boldly onto the church's turf, and the squatter must be put back in its own place. The government has grabbed chunks of moral truth and tradition from the church, saying, "We, rather than you, will decide." Under the rubric of antidiscrimination or the "right to privacy," the government has begun erasing the traditional bounds of marriage, denying the unborn the right to life, and pushing God and godly virtues to the fringes of public life. The government's attempt to shove the church away from these issues doesn't make them "political" or out of bounds for the church. These are still moral matters of the gravest concern, matters about which the church has a reason and an obligation to speak.

Some church leaders may say they do not want to involve their churches in "politics," but that is not how they respond when their own congregations are threatened.

In my town, a church located itself inside a storefront at a strip shopping center. The pastor had never been one to involve his church in social issues because he didn't think of himself as an "activist." That changed suddenly when an adult bookstore tried to move in next door. The city zoning law required that such a business locate at least 500 feet from any church facility, so the porno business erected a wooden fence between its proposed store and the church, running it straight out into the parking lot. This gimmick would force people to walk more than 500 feet to get from one to the other.

That was enough for this pastor. He got "political." He appeared several times before the city council. He asked his congregation to write letters and make phone calls. He recruited other Christians in the community to bring pressure on city leaders. Thankfully, the council ended the problem by passing a stronger zoning law.

Several years ago an atheist lawyer in Colorado Springs mounted a statewide campaign to remove the property tax exemptions from all nonprofit organizations in Colorado. His animosity was aimed at churches as well as the growing number of nonprofit religious organizations relocating to Colorado Springs, Focus on the Family chief among them. In order to seem fair, he lumped in every nonprofit agency: zoos, the opera, blood banks, the U.S. Olympic Training Center, private schools and colleges, soup kitchens, halfway houses, and many others. He was able to get enough signatures to put his measure on the ballot, which was a surprise to many people and a wake-up call for pastors.

Suddenly a broad-based coalition of nonprofit organizations began working to defeat the ballot initiative, for if it passed, many of the smaller organizations, including churches, would have to close. The measure was buried on Election Day, with 83 percent voting no. On this issue, most pastors had little problem getting into "politics" by talking about the measure from the pulpit (which was perfectly legal for them to do) and urging their congregations to vote against it. Some pastors even took up collections to help finance the campaign against the ballot measure.

In some parts of the country, such as the fast-growing Virginia suburbs adjacent to Washington, D.C., local zoning agencies are making it particularly difficult for churches to buy property. The result is that Christians have begun paying much closer attention to local politics, because so many of the churches have had to defend themselves against the belligerence of government officials.

Some might say in response that the churches *have* to engage in these limited activities to stay alive and functioning. They have no choice. That's true, and that is precisely the point. The churches have been involved in these kinds of things because their welfare is threatened. To those churches that get into "politics" or social action only when the well-being of a congregation is at stake, two things need to be said. First, it proves false the notion that churches don't get involved in "politics," for obviously they do. Second, to enter that arena only when a congregation's own health is at issue is very self-serving. A church concerned solely with itself isn't a church; it's a club or lodge. Jesus' admonition to be the salt in a decaying society and to be the light in that darkening world is a much stronger and broader call than simply waking up when a congregation finds its own neck on the block.

WHAT THE BIBLE SAYS

Pastors and teachers who decide to educate their congregations about the relationship of the church to the government have a rich vein of biblical truth to mine. The Bible is replete with commentary on the value of righteousness in public life and on the importance God has attached to the institution of government.

The book of Proverbs has much to say about the impact of godliness on culture. It tells us that "righteousness exalts a nation, but sin is a disgrace to any people" (Proverbs 14:34). It tells us that "through the blessing of the upright a city is exalted, but by the mouth of the wicked it is destroyed" (Proverbs 11:11). And it says that "when the righteous thrive, the people rejoice; when the wicked rule, the people groan" (Proverbs 29:2).

Christian people, as much as anyone else, constitute "the people." We have as much right to contend for our views as does any other citizen. And if we sit idly by while "the wicked rule," without doing what we can to change matters, then we, ultimately, are to blame.

The apostle Paul speaks significantly about this in his letter to the Romans. He devotes a passage to the relationship between Roman citizens who are Christians and their government. The passage is surprising, given that the government of Paul's day was thoroughly corrupt, and Paul is recommending that his Roman readers be good citizens. Paul writes:

There is no authority except that which God has established. The authorities that exist have been established by God. Consequently, he who rebels against the authority is rebelling against what God has instituted, and those who do so will bring judgment on themselves. For rulers hold no terror for those who do right, but for those who do wrong. Do you want to be free from fear of the one in authority? Then do what is right and he will commend you. For he is God's servant to do you good. But if you do wrong, be afraid, for he does not bear the sword for nothing. He is God's servant, an agent of wrath to bring punishment on the wrongdoer. Therefore, it is necessary to submit to the authorities, not only because of possible punishment but also because of conscience. (Romans 13:1-5)

Paul is saying that even secular authorities serve at God's pleasure, whether they acknowledge Him or not, and certainly the Roman despots did not. Paul also is saying that Christians are to be model citizens, for Christianity is a spiritual and moral movement, not an agency for political revolution. In our day, and in our country, our government derives its legitimacy from the consent of the people. If the people neglect the government, they are not respecting the governing authorities as Romans 13 commands.

What Caesar Demands

When Jewish religious leaders tried to back Jesus into a corner over whether they should pay taxes to Caesar, He replied by asking for a denarius, a coin of the Roman realm.

"Whose portrait is this?" Jesus asked. "And whose inscription?"

"Caesar's," they replied. Then Jesus said to them, "Give to Caesar what is Caesar's and to God what is God's" (Mark 12:17). The passage concludes by saying the Pharisees "were amazed at him."

And indeed they had a right to be amazed at this answer. The Roman army was despised in Israel, and the taxes that Jesus implied should be paid helped to keep the army in place. Furthermore, the Jewish turncoats who were in the employ of the Roman government to collect those taxes on behalf of Caesar were themselves extortionists, wringing whatever they could out of their fellow countrymen. Jesus was assenting to the people's participation in all of this.

In the United States today, "Caesar" still makes demands, but those demands make more sense because of the kind of country in which we live. We have an ordered society, a military capable of protecting our borders, local police and fire protection, clean water, paved roads, a dependable political system that will transfer power peacefully when administrations change. We have a functioning system of trade and commerce, with capital markets that allow businesses to be started and expanded.

We have much more to appreciate than did the Israelites in Jesus' day, and yet He asked the people to honor their governmental obligations. All the more should we, including a particular responsibility unknown to the Jews of Jesus' day. Our government asks for our participation. We have a government "of the people, by the people and for the people," in Lincoln's memorable phrase. We Christians have a duty as citizens to lend our government our involvement.

The threshold responsibility of a citizen is to vote, and all churches ought to encourage their members to register and cast votes intelligently. But they seldom do, and there is no evidence that Christians vote in any greater percentages than non-Christians. The fact is that voting participation by all citizens continues to slide. In 1998, only 45 percent of those eligible to cast votes did so, and that was down from 48 percent just two years previously.[1] If churches acted responsibly in this matter, they could have a significant impact on the election results in their communities and on the nation as a whole.

A caution here: It is illegal for churches to participate in activity for or against a candidate for public office. It is a much different matter, however, simply to encourage church members to register and to vote. Not only is this fully legal but in fact our moral obligation as citizens requires it, and God has called us to it in Christ's admonition to honor the governing authorities.

BEYOND THE THRESHOLD

But casting an informed vote is only the first obligation of the citizen who is a Christian. Those who have been blessed with the personal gifts of a gracious personality, diplomacy, enthusiasm, and drive, as well as having an interest in public affairs, are the people who ought to be encouraged by their local church to step out and run for office.

Sadly, churches seldom do this, either. The idea of public office as a calling to a mission field is absent from most churches, and that is a shame. For in few other fields of endeavor will a Christian get to know and work as closely with people whose deepest beliefs are alien to their own. The proper role for the Christian citizen is to participate in government as fully as his calling and skills can take him, whether it be limited to voting or as an active government leader. When the sparks fly over moral issues in the councils of government, how much more effective it is (and honoring to Christ) to have skilled Christian people at the center of the debate, in full possession of the facts and a record of public trust. Sometimes, of course, this isn't enough, and the moral position is defeated. But many times the impact of Christian leaders on difficult moral issues has been astounding.

Win or lose, this is a much preferred scenario to the one in which the Christian side of the issue is represented by a protest group marching outside and waving Bibles and picket signs, totally absent from the decision-making process. Christianity is no mere protest movement. In our country, the blessings of liberty were secured for all, and Christian people have equal opportunity to set good public policy, not merely to protest after bad policy has been set.

"I'LL RESPOND WHEN THEY COME FOR ME"

Some pastors and elders who steadfastly oppose involvement in "politics" or social action say that if the government should ever become oppressive and seek to prevent the church from worshiping God, then they will simply resist the government and accept whatever tribulations come their way.

This is an astonishing statement. It says that churches should make the great leap from isolation to civil disobedience, with all the attendant threats: prosecutions, heavy fines, risks of jail sentences, confiscation of property, adverse media, and interruption of ministry. Civil disobedience is the last resort, not the only resort.

A church leader who adopts that view owes it to his congregation to explain it fully, for without question there will be members of the congregation who won't agree. Some will think it more prudent to try to extinguish the fire before it engulfs the house.

A pastor who believes that his congregation can simply sit out the culture war and then somehow resist at the end is foolish. He has squandered his call as protector of his flock, he has dishonored his role as a moral leader in his community, and he has ignored the plain meaning of Scripture, as it applies to our life in a free, democratic society.

WHAT LIES AHEAD

While some leaders dither about how to respond to the madness afoot in society, and while other leaders argue that we should simply keep quiet and preach and evangelize, there are secular forces intent on chewing away at the ability of the church to do even that much. For example, a group called Soulforce, which protests the annual denominational conferences of churches that will not condone same-sex marriage, has its members wear shirts bearing the slogan "Stop Spiritual Violence." By "violence" they mean merely preaching on those passages of Scripture that speak against the practice of homosexuality. They claim that the church's stand against homosexuality encourages people to hate homosexuals and commit actual violence against them, and that only when pastors decline to preach on those passages of the Bible will homosexuals be safe.

The label of "violence" has begun to extend even to Christian evangelism. A group of left-wing religious leaders in Chicago asked that the annual Southern Baptist Convention not be held in their city in June 2000, because the evangelizing done by the Southern Baptists could spark violence against Jews, Hindus, and Muslims. The preaching of God's Word could produce a climate conducive to hate crimes, said the group, which called itself the Council of Religious Leaders of Metropolitan Chicago. The president of the Southern Baptists, Paige Patterson, correctly asserted that it is a small step from saying that Christ's message *produces* hate crimes to saying that Christ's message *is* a hate crime. The convention was held in Chicago without incident.

Some church leaders, not wanting to sound "intolerant," are beginning to make accommodations to the many secular pressures bearing in upon the church. If they simply continue in this fashion without responding to these forces, then we are consigning our children and grandchildren to live in a country that will have grown cold and harsh, where the morally blind rule the day and where the most atrocious ideas are advanced in the most matter-of-fact manner.

For the church to say it should sit by and not get into the "politics" of controversies such as this is to fail at Jesus' admonition to be salt and light. The issues facing American life today are issues of righteousness, and the country desperately needs the church's transcendent voice. By the time society realizes this, it may be too late for that voice to do any good. But now is the time for the church to enter the debate, for never before have so many people been so confused.

CHAPTER SIX

Shine Your Light, Embrace Your World

"BLESSED ARE THOSE," SAID JESUS, "who hunger and thirst for righteousness, for they will be filled" (Matthew 5:6). As I noted in chapter four, righteousness is everything that is right. It is the standard of God, in belief and action. The first and most important act of righteousness is becoming right with God, and God accomplished that for believers through His Son. But righteousness also means standing for right against wrong, in personal and cultural behavior, because the way of God is the way of love for the people He created.

In his reflection on the Beatitudes, commentator William Barclay says that few modern people really know what it means to hunger and thirst, because we live in the midst of so much material well-being. However, for the people in Palestine who made up Christ's audience that day, hunger and thirst were very real problems. The workingman was never far from hunger, so meager were his wages and so uncertain were the weather, the crops, and the economy. Likewise, any traveler in that hot, desolate climate faced the prospect of severe dehydration, thanks to the burning sun and unrelenting wind that swirled the sand in a suffocating cloud, parching his throat. Barclay writes:

> So then, the hunger which this beatitude describes is no genteel hunger which could be satisfied with a mid-morning snack; the thirst of which it speaks is no thirst which could be slaked with a cup of coffee or an iced drink. It is the hunger of

the man who is starving for food, and the thirst of the man who will die unless he drinks.... In effect [this Beatitude] demands, "How much do you want goodness? Do you want it as much as a starving man wants food, and as much as a man dying of thirst wants water?" How intense is our desire for goodness?[1]

That, then, is the intensity with which Christ asks us to cling to, and act upon, godly righteousness. Four verses later, Jesus commented on the results of this kind of passion: "Blessed are those who are persecuted because of righteousness, for theirs is the kingdom of heaven" (Matthew 5:10).

These words, conveying the uncomfortable truth that trouble lay ahead, must have unsettled His audience. For Jesus dropped the more generic "blessed are *those*" in order to put aside all doubt about whom He was speaking to. "Blessed are *you*," He said, "when people insult you, persecute you and falsely say all kinds of evil against you because of me. Rejoice and be glad, because great is your reward in heaven, for in the same way they persecuted the prophets who were before you" (Matthew 5:11-12, emphasis added).

SALT AND LIGHT

Jesus left no doubt that this hunger for righteousness should change the world. He went on to say:

> You are the salt of the earth. But if the salt loses its saltiness, how can it be made salty again? It is no longer good for anything, except to be thrown out and trampled by men.
>
> You are the light of the world. A city on a hill cannot be hidden. Neither do people light a lamp and put it under a bowl. Instead they put it on its stand, and it gives light to everyone in the house. In the same way, let your light shine before men, that they may see your good deeds and praise your Father in heaven. (Matthew 5:13-16)

This is the Master's call to be salt and light in society. Salt prevents decay when it is rubbed into meat. But its preservative trait works only when it penetrates the food, and it becomes useless if adulterated by other chemical substances. It must remain pure if it is to accomplish its task. Jesus' illustration is profound because it demonstrates that Christians are to penetrate society while keeping themselves from being penetrated.

We usually make one of two mistakes. The first is to try so hard to avoid contamination by the culture that we are like salt forever left in the saltshaker. It never accomplishes its purposes. For most of the past century, this has been the problem of the evangelical, Bible-believing churches.

The second mistake is to allow ourselves to become "unsalty." Christians become polluted by the world and then have nothing to say to the worldly. This is often the plight of Sunday morning worshipers who hear sermons in church but allow themselves to be watered down by secular influences throughout the rest of the week. They are useless in penetrating society, for society has penetrated them.

The pastor and theologian John Stott wrote plainly about what it means to be the salt of the earth:

> To begin with, we Christians should be more courageous, more outspoken in condemning evil. Condemnation is negative, to be sure, but the action of salt is negative. Sometimes standards slip and slide in a community for want of a clear Christian protest. Luther makes much of this, emphasizing that denunciation and proclamation go hand in hand when the gospel is truly preached.... Too often evangelical Christians have interpreted their social responsibility in terms only of helping the casualties of a sick society, and have done nothing to change the structures which cause the casualties. Just as doctors are concerned not only with the treatment of patients but also with preventive medicine and public health, so we should concern ourselves with what might be called preventive social medicine and higher standards of moral hygiene.... As Sir Frederick Catherwood put it,... "To try to improve society is not worldliness but love. To wash your hands of society is not love but worldliness."[2]

Jesus' challenge to His followers to be the "light of the world" is powerful and unmistakably clear. Light penetrates darkness. Light conquers darkness. The absence of light is what defines darkness. To know the truth and yet be afraid of standing for the truth is as nonsensical, Jesus says, as lighting a lamp and putting it under a basket. Light is meant to shine in the darkness.

Today's society is decaying, and the darkness of secular life grows. In circumstances like these, the witness of Christians should be noticeable, and it is quite natural at times that it will be controversial. If it is not—if Christians are coasting along in perfect contentment with the state of things or are blissfully ignorant of current events—then Christ's powerful metaphors of salt and light mean nothing to them. They miss the full scope of what it means to be Christian. This is particularly true in an era like our own, when the preserving chemistry of salt and the illumination of divine light are so desperately needed.

Sometimes our Bible commentators don't help much, for they tend to offer a pinched view of these Bible passages. Many such authors provide examples of what it means to be salt in society today, and their illustrations usually center on the same situation. It is that of a conversation among friends or coworkers. The talk turns to lewd jokes or lascivious gossip, but the conversation is cut short when a Christian walks by, because everyone knows the Christian would not approve.[3]

Do salt and light really mean no more than that? Perhaps back when Judeo-Christian morality was the predominant view in our society, it was easier to view this passage from the Sermon on the Mount merely as an admonition to respectable personal behavior. Today, however, we are in a new era, and Jesus' words have begun to take on new meaning.

Some years ago, Deb and I went on a cruise in the Caribbean. Our very first activity was a lifeboat drill. We didn't actually embark on the lifeboats, but we were shown where to gather should the need arise, and we practiced putting on life vests. Since we hadn't even left port, the threat of sinking was remote, and the lifeboat drill held little interest. But if the drill had been conducted in blustery winds and heaving seas on the open ocean, all of us would have been much more attentive.

Today, the cultural seas are heaving and the sky threatens, so the mechanisms designed to preserve life—those of God's righteousness—should take on new significance. We are blessed people as Christians living in the United States. We have the same rights as any other citizens to advance our ideas and influence the course of our laws and public policy. Because the need for Christian influence is so great in our era, the concept of salt and light must encompass this larger involvement.

Suppose a "Society of Liars" organized for the purpose of striking down those "old, outmoded" laws against lying under oath in court. Let's say its members claimed that the perjury laws discriminate against those who believe lying is okay. Would we concede that laws against lying shouldn't be "imposed" on everyone? Or would we, with some resignation, begin to lay out the case against lying?

Put that way, it's an easy call. But the same goes for any other moral issue. Being salt and light in this age means contending responsibly for godly standards wherever they are under assault. This explains why there is no truth to the cliché that you shouldn't mix religion and politics. That tired slogan is usually offered by those in politics who resent having moral pressure brought against them. Or it is voiced by religious people who don't like the discomfort of exposing their deepest beliefs to ridicule and rejection. There is no escaping the mixture of religion and politics, because nearly every law is the result of someone's judgment about what is good and what is bad.

Still, you often hear the same objections raised over and over. Let's address several of them.

"What about the separation of church and state?" The protection afforded to religion in the First Amendment to the Constitution is nearly absolute. Regarding religion, the amendment says, first, that there should be no establishment of a national religion, and second, that there shall be no law inhibiting the free exercise of religion. The First Amendment statement about establishment was intended only to ensure that no single Christian denomination became the official church of the new nation. This was a general concern, because several of the new states had their own officially established denominations, and one of the driving forces in the creation of the United States was the desire to be free from the king of England and his officially sanctioned Anglican church.

As our country developed, and as our courts interpreted the meaning of the new constitution, there was never a problem with the public expression of faith. In fact, faith in God was universally seen as a valuable source of order and gentility for the good of all. In the country's founding era, there were no real public schools, only church schools, and as the public school system gradually developed, the traditions of church schools were freely borrowed. Students prayed and memorized Bible verses.

This did not change until the twentieth century, when decisions by the federal courts began to diminish the free exercise clause and turn the establishment clause into a battering ram of grotesque proportions, knocking down public "establishment" wherever the courts sensed it. At first it meant there could no longer be prayers or Bible reading in public schools. But it didn't stop there. Today this unfortunate interpretation of the First Amendment has come to mean there can be no prayers offered by students at school athletic contests or graduation ceremonies. Nor can there be Nativity scenes on public property, or the Ten Commandments posted in school classrooms. Atheists have successfully used the courts to remove all references to God from the mottoes and insignias of cities and towns.

Over the years, the secularizing trend of the courts has turned public schools into an ever bleaker moral arena. Yet parents who are increasingly dissatisfied with those schools have been forbidden by the courts from using their tax dollars to send their children to private schools whose values reflect their own. The children may leave, the courts have said, but their parents' tax money must remain behind with the public school system.

"Aren't we just trying to impose our views on everyone?" This is but another cliché. The charge is often made against people who cite moral truth as the reason some things are right and others are wrong. But it is an argument that falls quickly. In a republic like ours, no one can illegitimately "impose" anything on anyone. Only a tyrant can do that. Moral

people can *contend* for their views along with everyone else. Laws that declare certain things right and other things wrong are passed by freely elected legislators, and we're thankful that many of our laws are codifications of widely accepted moral truths. Laws prohibit stealing, lying under oath (perjury), murder, assault, destroying another's property, etc. All these laws are part of society's official recognition that good and evil exist. None of these laws was imposed.

Actually, in our day, there *is* one arena in which laws can be said to have been "imposed," but Christians aren't the ones doing it. Our state and federal courts have been rendering opinions that never would have been authorized by the public had they been given the opportunity to weigh in.

For example, the controversy over whether same-sex couples can be married did not arise because conservatives imposed their beliefs on society. It arose because the Vermont Supreme Court ordered the state legislature to grant same-sex couples the same benefits given to all married couples. Such a law never would have passed had the people of Vermont been given a chance to vote on the issue, nor would the legislature have acted without the court's twisting its arm. In light of this controversy, most state legislatures have now explicitly acted to limit marriage to one man and one woman. Previously many of these states had rather vague laws failing to specify that only a man and a woman could be married, because any other arrangement had been unthinkable.

The issue of prayer in public schools is still controversial, but not because religious people imposed their values on the country. The courts imposed a prohibition, as we have just seen, against the will of a vast majority of people who want it restored.

Abortion battles rage throughout national politics today not because pro-life people imposed their values on the country. The debate exists because of the Supreme Court's *Roe v. Wade* decision in 1973, in which the court decided that every one of the state laws placing limits on abortions somehow violated a "right to privacy."

Homosexuality is a controversial issue today not because of an epidemic of hate toward gays but because activists have used a small number of reprehensible acts of violence against homosexuals to press for a government-imposed "normalization" of the homosexual lifestyle. This movement, breathtaking in its audacity and aided by a number of favorable court decisions, is steamrolling over the moral traditions of Western civilization. All objections are labeled as "hate" and used as further evidence that more government action is needed.

(Although gay activists often speak of rampant hate toward them, the data show otherwise. Each year the FBI releases statistics on hate crimes it gathers from local police agencies. In 1998, the FBI took reports from 10,730 police agencies representing 46 states and the District of Columbia. There were 1,260 incidents of hate crimes against homosexuals, intimidation being the most common. That's fewer than one incident for every seven police agencies that reported. There were more reported incidents of hate crimes based on a person's religion than on his sexual orientation.)

To the extent that anyone is "imposing" views on other people, it is the political Left, as it adeptly brings legal cases before sympathetic, unelected judges. These cases unravel centuries of settled traditions. That is a major reason for the social turmoil we see all about us today.

"But you can't legislate morality." Most laws are, in fact, founded on moral decisions. When people say, "You can't legislate morality," they probably mean there is a limit to how effective laws are in bringing people to act rightly. That's true, but we still need laws against murder or any other serious violation of God's standards.

Admittedly, we can't force anyone to acknowledge God or willingly obey Him. But like it or not, they either have to accept God's ideas about what's right and wrong or pay the consequences. We've just said that biblical morality—no lying, cheating, stealing, murdering, etc.—is good for society, and we should be pleased that our forefathers had enough sense to translate these godly principles into laws. Those principles work well for everybody, because they reflect what is true about human nature.

Today, the side that doesn't want God's standards to prevail has the upper hand on some issues and has begun passing laws and angling for court decisions that reflect immoral standards. When societal norms are determined without reference to biblical absolutes, they become grotesque. This is where we are on the issue of abortion. Look at part of a recent newspaper story:

> CORPUS CHRISTI, Tex.—A man who drove drunk into a pregnant woman's car was convicted today of killing the woman's baby, who was born a month and a half premature because of the crash. Jurors were not required to consider whether Krystal Zuniga was a person or a fetus at the time of the accident.[4]

Undoubtedly, little Krystal's mother wanted her to be born, so it was a great tragedy when the unborn child was killed in the crash. But our courts have said that women may kill their unborn children if they wish, without penalty. Those babies are not persons. It depends on what the mother wants. To get around this great moral confusion, the judge in this case told the jury that they didn't have to trifle over details, such as just what Krystal was—an unborn child or a piece of meat.

This is barbarian. It is reminiscent of the ancient Romans who watched as gladiators tore each other apart in the arena. A fallen fighter would await a thumbs-up or thumbs-down from the spectators (and sometimes the emperor) to determine whether he would receive mercy or be finished off. His life hung from one thread only—the fancy of the crowd. A society that behaves according to ungodly morals is a cold and brutal place. And that is what we are becoming.

THE SLIPPERY SLOPE

The slide away from biblical morality doesn't stop. It just gets worse and worse. The people who agree with the slogan "You can't legislate morality" don't understand this, so they fall for a ruse. They keep their beliefs to themselves. But their opponents, whose notions of morality don't include God's ideas, certainly don't stop.

For example, during the 1990s, Congress was trying to put a slight restriction on the practice of abortion. The majority wanted to eliminate only one kind of abortion, the most barbaric procedure ever devised. It is called partial-birth abortion. The procedure entails the delivery of a late-term baby, all except the head, which remains in the uterus while the rest of the child, alive and kicking, is held in the doctor's hand. He plunges a scissors into the base of the technically still-undelivered head and inserts a catheter to suck out the baby's brains, collapsing the skull and making it possible to pull the head from the uterus.

During debate over this procedure in the Senate, Senator Rick Santorum of Pennsylvania, the leader of the campaign to declare the practice illegal, was engaged in a debate with Senator Barbara Boxer of California, the Senate champion for partial-birth abortion. At one point in their debate came this chilling exchange:

> SANTORUM: I would like to ask you this question. You agree, once the child is born, separated from the mother, that the child is protected by the Constitution and cannot be killed. Do you agree with that?
> BOXER: I think when you bring your baby home, when your baby is born,... the baby belongs to your family and has rights.[5]

Can this be true? Does a baby become a baby when its parents leave the hospital with it? Santorum wanted to know if Boxer really believed that, so he asked:

> SANTORUM: Obviously you don't mean they have to take the baby out of the hospital for it to be protected by the Constitution. Once the baby is separated from the mother, you would agree—completely separated from the mother—you would agree that baby is entitled to constitutional protection?
> BOXER: I don't want to engage in this. You had the same conversation with a colleague of mine, and I never saw such a twisting of his remarks.[6]

In writing about this exchange, law professor Hadley Arkes notes that pro-abortionists believe human beings have no inherent rights until they are assigned those rights by the parents. Santorum put the question so plainly that Boxer ducked away rather than admit to this jarring belief: The right to abortion is the right to a dead child, even if the killing amounts to infanticide.

This is no loose thread in the fabric of pro-abortionist thought. In 1998, Princeton University caused a sensation when it hired Peter Singer to be a bioethics professor at its University Center for Human Values. Singer's beliefs are fully consistent with the implied beliefs of Barbara Boxer in her debate with Santorum. Singer teaches that newborn children do not achieve personhood until that distinction is assigned by the parents, and Singer believes the parents ought to have some time to decide the question.

The pro-life position—that life begins at conception, giving the unborn person a right to the full protection of law—has been checked by the hostile court decisions that started with *Roe v. Wade* in 1973. This has allowed the pro-abortion philosophy to grow and develop unchecked. That is why, at the turn of the new millennium, a man like Singer can be embraced by one of our major universities.

STILL TIME TO ACT

In the basement floor of my house, in an out-of-the-way corner of our family room, there is a sump. A sump is a pit in the floor, about the size of a curbside garbage can. It is a shallow well into which water flows from a drainpipe laid along the bottom, outside edge of the foundation.

Most sumps have pumps to expel the water through a second pipe leading out to the street. But mine has no pump and no pipe. The builder explained that our foundation sits high, so water would not collect in the sump. Therefore, no need for a pump and no need for that second pipe.

And he was right—for the first few years we lived in the house. Eventually I began hearing a drip, drip, drip in the family room after rainstorms. Water was finding its way into the drainpipe and trickling into the sump. After a year or two of this, I opened the lid and saw that the sump was about half full. *Shouldn't have to do anything for another couple of years,* I told myself. I shut the lid and forgot about it.

One spring, the rain was unusually heavy. For days it poured. I received a frantic call from Deb on one of those rainy afternoons. She had gone downstairs to find water pouring in through the window wells, which were fast filling up with water. One corner of the carpet was already soaked, and the water was spreading fast. More ominously, across the family room, near the furniture and the piano, water was gushing into the sump as if a water spigot had been turned on full blast.

A friend and I started bailing, using two five-gallon buckets at a time, just as the sump began to overflow onto the carpet. Deb began calling stores to find a pump. By working furiously, we managed to keep the water level just shy of overflow (and me just shy of a heart attack), but only by lugging 20 gallons of water at a time up the stairs and out to the street. Deb returned with one of the last pumps to be found, hooked it up to the garden hose, and strung the hose through the window and out to the street.

How much easier it would have been to solve the sump problem when I first began hearing that drip, drip, drip. Had I tackled the problem early on, there would have been no flooded carpet, no maniacal bailing with the heavy buckets, and no stress.

Why do we put off little problems until they become big ones? Choose your answer; there are many. "Too busy with life" sums it up for most of us. Little problems creep up on us, and before we even notice them, they're gushers. Nothing is easier than ignoring the drip, drip, drip of problems on the periphery of our lives.

Things are going wrong in society today on many fronts. We seem to be eroding gradually, drip by drip by drip. But so far, thankfully, on most fronts there has been no flood of destruction. Culture is on the slippery slope, to be sure, but it doesn't seem to have hit bottom. For most Americans, some things are still right, just not as many as before. And some things are wrong, although not as few as before. We're living on the cultural deposits of moral wisdom made by earlier generations. It is still possible to live a productive life, be part of a church, and raise kids. It's just best not to watch too much news, or to inquire too deeply about what the kids are being taught in public schools, or to consider what the professors are teaching on college campuses.

Yet we cannot keep our heads in the sand this way, because the responsibility given to us by God is immense. His command is to do whatever is right, and to do so by acting as salt and light—two metaphors that do not allow for timidity or isolation from the world around us. And He has commanded us to undertake these bold measures for a reason that is far more significant than most Christians have ever grasped: God has assigned us to be nothing less than the caretakers of His creation.

CHAPTER SEVEN

Creation—Our Assignment from God

ONCE I SAW A T-SHIRT THAT READ: "Obey Gravity. It's the Law!"

Funny how some laws don't require policemen.

When we think of gravity, we think of something normal and natural. It's so ordinary that we hardly reflect on it at all. The law of gravity doesn't usually make us think about God, and the theologian John Stott tells us that's a problem—we forget that God is the God of all nature as well as of religion. Stott writes, "Our God is often too small because He is too religious."[1] We believe, says Stott, that He is found only in church and that the creation, which He pronounced "good," ended at the borders of the Garden of Eden.

One weekend our youngest daughter, Beth, and I went on a backpacking trip into the Colorado Rocky Mountains with some friends. How beautiful it was to see the summer sky and the sunlit forests in high, clear altitude! I hardly noticed that I had cut my arm on a bush along the trail. The next morning we hiked into a canyon and fished in a lake fed from a waterfall cascading down from a snowfield that still hugged the canyon wall in late July. I had forgotten completely about that cut on my arm, which by now had begun to heal.

Had there been with us that beautiful day a man named Michael Behe, he might have told me that I was enjoying the wrong scenery if I really wanted to appreciate the glory of creation. Behe is a biochemist at Lehigh University and has written a book about those finely calibrated miniature machines called human cells.[2] Part of his book is devoted to an explanation of how blood manages to form clots whenever the skin is broken. It is a process in which 32 proteins, each composed of blood cells, march in precise order to the scene of the wound, and each protein performs a highly specialized task that builds the body's bulwark against infection—a scab. If any one of those 32 proteins arrives at the scene too early or too late, the blood would fail to clot. Evolutionists cannot begin to offer an explanation for the lowly scab, says Behe.

CREATION IS MORE THAN WE IMAGINE

Well, even after reading Behe's book, I find that I still want to gaze at lakes rather than at scabs. But I do see that God's creation is more profound and encompassing than I had previously thought. All of us have difficulty appreciating everything that God has done and continues to do.

It isn't hard to see how the meaning of *creation* has become so limited. When we speak about God creating the world, we naturally think of the six days of creation in the book of Genesis. In the great debate over creationism versus evolution, the argument centers on what happened a long time ago, not what is happening today.

But when one puts that word *creation* under a scriptural magnifying glass, one sees God's fingerprints everywhere. He is in charge of current events, not just of plants and animals and the natural laws. Just as gravity happens, so does God stay involved in His creation.

And that's not all. The theologian Albert M. Wolters explains that just as a human ruler does certain tasks himself and delegates other tasks to subordinates, God has done the same. He Himself established the order of the universe, the rotations of stars and planets, and the rhythms of the resulting seasons and weather patterns. These are things the Creator has accomplished without the help of mankind. But other tasks He has delegated to human beings. These include making tools and cultivating crops, advancing the sciences by learning ever more about the complex processes of God's creation, uplifting people's spirits by developing aesthetically pleasing art, and learning how to live together by importing God's concepts of justice into the routines of everyday life.

PEOPLE: THE CARETAKERS OF CREATION

Admittedly, in Old Testament times, the weather patterns and seasons of planting and harvest made it easier for people to think of God, because they were so dependent on nature for their livelihood. Today our modern conveniences allow us to treat the effects of rain and sun, the winter's heat and the summer's cold, as minor pleasures or hindrances.

There is something deeper to the rhythms of nature, something we shouldn't fail to see. The dependability of the natural world exemplifies God's faithfulness to mankind. "As long as the earth endures, seedtime and harvest, cold and heat, summer and winter, day and night will never cease" (Genesis 8:22). That promise was made to Noah and his family after the Flood receded. Ever since, the rhythm of nature signals the presence of God, the keeper of promises.

But there was more said by God to Noah on that significant day when the great Flood abated. He commanded that Noah and his descendants should begin to take possession and control of the natural world:

> Then God blessed Noah and his sons, saying to them, "Be fruitful and increase in number and fill the earth. The fear and dread of you will fall upon all the beasts of the earth and all the birds of the air.... They are given into your hands. Everything that lives and moves will be food for you. Just as I gave you the green plants, now I give you everything." (Genesis 9:1-3)

In a stunning assignment of responsibility, God said He would someday demand an accounting not merely of how man dealt with the animal kingdom but also of how he cared for God's most precious creature, man himself: "For your lifeblood I will surely demand an accounting" (Genesis 9:5a). People matter so much to God that a man who ends the life of another would forfeit his own life, and God transferred *that* awesome responsibility to man in the same moment: "Whoever sheds the blood of man, by man shall his blood be shed; for in the image of God has God made man" (Genesis 9:6).

The truth is that God has transferred control over significant aspects of His creation to man, and He will demand an answer for how well man has handled this responsibility.

In our day, we have made an unfortunate separation. We can see how certain laws must be obeyed. A person who steps from the upper ledge of a building will fall, so we respect the law of gravity. Birds fly south for the winter and bears hibernate, because each is compelled by the laws of instinct that guide their lives. But for those laws that guide people in the nurturing of their families and communities, and in the system of justice that determines whether men will be punished for their transgressions, we have strayed horribly. We don't see—not even as Christians—that laws for productive living come from God and should be honored.

We humans have paid a dear price for our failure to obey God's laws for living. In 1997, there were 1.16 million divorces in the United States, and the number of cohabiting couples has increased 1,000 percent in the last three decades. It is not surprising, then, that child abuse and neglect have soared. As we willfully disobey God's laws for people, tragedy ensues, just as surely as it does for a person who disobeys God's law of gravity and steps off the ledge.

PHYSICAL LAWS AND SOCIAL LAWS—ALL ARE GOD'S

Wolters points out that "there is no essential difference, it would seem, between God's word of command to snow and ice and his command to his people.... They belong to his universal law for all creation,"[3] even though God gives man a choice as to whether he will carry out the laws for civilized living. As it says in Psalm 147:15-20:

> He sends his command to the earth;
>   his word runs swiftly.
> He spreads the snow like wool
>   and scatters the frost like ashes.
> He hurls down his hail like pebbles.
>   Who can withstand his icy blast?

He sends his word and melts them;
   he stirs up his breezes, and the waters flow.
He has revealed his word to Jacob,
   his laws and decrees to Israel.
He has done this for no other nation;
   they do not know his laws.

God's laws, whether those that govern the physical world or those that govern society, are good and should be obeyed. The New Testament is quite clear about this, and in several places it identifies aspects of His creation that are not part of the physical world yet must be honored just as any other creation of God. Marriage is one of them. Paul warns Timothy against a heresy that forbids marriage, reminding him that "everything God created is good, and nothing is to be rejected" (1 Timothy 4:4).

Likewise, Paul admonishes Christians to obey the Roman government, and he does so by connecting human government to God's creation. "Everyone must submit himself to the governing authorities, for there is no authority except that which God has established. The authorities that exist have been established by God. Consequently, he who rebels against the authority is rebelling against what God has instituted" (Romans 13:1-2).

The apostle Peter says this even more plainly: "Submit yourself for the Lord's sake to every *authority instituted* among men" (1 Peter 2:13, emphasis added). Wolters notes that the italicized words translate the Greek word *ktisis,* the usual word for "creation" or "creature." He says, "It seems plain, therefore, that civil authority belongs to the created order; the state is founded in an ordinance of God."[4] What an arresting thought! God's creation includes the great cities—Calcutta, New York, Mexico City—as much as it does the stunning sunset and the emerald sea.

We used to believe this a lot more than we do today. Early in our nation's history, the Founding Fathers were quite specific about the connection between God and government. In his first inaugural address as president, George Washington said, "We ought to be no less persuaded that the propitious smiles of heaven can never be expected on a nation that disregards the eternal rules of order and right which heaven itself has ordained."[5] Likewise, our second president, John Adams, said, "Religion and virtue are the only foundations, not only of republicanism and all free government, but of social felicity under all governments and in all the combinations of human society."[6] These are remarkably insightful comments on the fact that government is part of God's created order. What a shame that political leaders today are less cognizant of the connection and that those who are aware of it are fearful of stating it this boldly!

GOD SPEAKS PLAINLY TO ALL PEOPLE

The Bible, then, tells us that both material things (planets, stars, etc.) and nonmaterial things (marriage, government) are part of God's created order. The Bible also tells us that people don't need the Bible to understand this:

> The heavens declare the glory of God;
>   the skies proclaim the work of his hands.
> Day after day they pour forth speech;
>   night after night they display knowledge.
> There is no speech or language
>   where their voice is not heard.
> Their voice goes out into all the earth,
>   their words to the ends of the world. (Psalm 19:1-4)

The natural world testifies to the God who created all things; to all people, whatever their language and cultural beliefs, the heavenly creation "pours forth" knowledge about God.

Paul reiterates this truth in the New Testament. When he was in Lystra, the local citizens wanted to worship him and Barnabas as pagan gods. Paul admonished them to stop seeking after false gods and to worship instead "the living God, who made heaven and earth and sea and everything in them" (Acts 14:15). Paul went on to describe this God: "He has not left himself without testimony: He has shown kindness by giving you rain from heaven and crops in their seasons; he provides you with plenty of food and fills your hearts with joy" (Acts 14:17).

In his letter to Christians in Rome, Paul insists that all men know the truth. But they willfully resist it, and the wrath that comes upon them is their own fault:

> What may be known about God is plain to them, because God has made it plain to them. For since the creation of the world God's invisible qualities—his eternal power and divine nature—have been clearly seen, being understood from what has been made, so that men are without excuse. (Romans 1:19-20)

THE INTOLERANCE OF TOLERANCE

Some critics of Christians who are active in public affairs level the charge that Christians want to impose their views on everyone and create a theocracy in which God, not our elected representatives, is in charge. These secularists claim that if Christians had their way, the United States would become another Iran, led by Christian ayatollahs. The passages of Scripture I just quoted explain why this isn't true. The New Testament says all people have "the requirements of the law ... written on their hearts, their consciences also bearing witness" (Romans 2:15). Therefore, regardless of what people think about God, they can discern the difference between right and wrong, and so all can participate in government. Just as one can reject God and still respect His law of gravity, so one can reject God and still respect His laws for an orderly society. This "natural" law, if you will, based on what is best for human nature, is what Christians strive for. We do not want to create a theocracy.

In our day, when so many people are turning away from God, it is remarkable that so much of His created order still finds its way to the surface, just as it says in Romans. For example, many people today claim there is no such thing as absolute truth. When they say this, they are denying the existence of God's moral standard, of right and wrong, which is part of His created order. C. S. Lewis reminds us in his classic book *Mere Christianity* that people may claim to hold this view, but they really do not live their lives this way.

> Everyone has heard people quarrelling.... They say things like this: "How'd you like it if anyone did the same to you?"— "That's my seat, I was there first."—"Leave him alone, he isn't doing you any harm."...
>
> Now what interests me about these remarks is that the person who makes them is not merely saying that the other man's behaviour does not happen to please him. He is appealing to some kind of standard of behaviour which he expects the other man to know about. And the other man very seldom replies: "To hell with your standard." Nearly always he tries to make out that what he has been doing does not really go against the standard, or that if it does there is some special excuse.... It looks, in fact, very much as if both parties had in mind some kind of Law or Rule of fair play or decent behaviour or morality or whatever you like to call it, about which they really agreed.[7]

And in fact, Lewis writes, there is a universal law of fair play, or justice. Cultures may differ over the details but not on the major points. In the history of the world, there has never been a country where men are rewarded for running away in battle, or where a man is rewarded for double-crossing his friends. "Selfishness has never been admired," Lewis writes. "Men have differed as to whether you should have one wife or four, but they have always agreed that you must not simply have any woman you liked."[8]

To hear people talk today, one would think that the only absolute standard is "tolerance," that there is no absolute right and wrong, and that we are to accept all viewpoints as equally valid. This, of course, is a recipe for social chaos. People really don't believe anything goes; it is a result of shallow thinking in our age. And in fact, those on the political Left today who claim to be "tolerant" are actually the most intolerant of all. Opposition to homosexual behavior, for example, no matter how compassionately expressed, is regarded by them as "hate speech," and

Christian preaching on this subject is called "spiritual violence." There is little effort to disagree intelligently with the Christian position; they wish only to eradicate it by the use of these demonizing labels.

GOD'S ETERNAL WISDOM

There is a universal norm for right behavior. Call it what you like: natural law, truth, common sense, or (as some derisively call it today) "intolerance." The standard for behavior is "written on the hearts of men," the Bible tells us, and it has been there for all time. The Bible calls it wisdom and says this about it:

> The LORD brought me forth as the first of his works,
>   before his deeds of old;
> I was appointed from eternity,
>   from the beginning, before the world began.
> I was there ... when he marked out the foundations of the earth.
> Then I was the craftsman at his side....
> Now then, my sons, listen to me;
>   blessed are those who keep my ways.
> Listen to my instruction and be wise;
>   do not ignore it.
> For whoever finds me finds life
>   and receives favor from the LORD.
> But whoever fails to find me harms himself;
>   all who hate me love death.
> (Proverbs 8:22-23, 27, 29-30, 32-33, 35-36)

God's standards apply to everyone; they infuse all people with an innate sense of right and wrong, as Scripture testifies. It is part of God's created order, an order that began with the events of Genesis chapter 1 but certainly didn't conclude there. In the first six days of creation, God formed the physical world, and He furnished it with plants, animals, and man. The laws governing this physical world are reflexive and instinctive.

Plants multiply, weather patterns change, birds migrate, all in predictable ways. These laws, says Albert Wolters, are "immediate." They are obeyed without question.

But at the close of the initial creation, God steps back and allows mankind to come to the fore, continuing the process of creation as it flowers into civilization. Man governs by principles that come from God, but these principles are not "immediate"—that is to say, people aren't made to obey God's laws instinctively. We have a choice in the matter. These laws are "mediate," because man is the mediator of whether to govern according to God's wisdom or his own. God has granted him the freedom to decide whether to obey what is written on his heart.

The task God has given man to continue the work of creation is significant, even though he is free to turn his back on it. "Be fruitful and increase in number; fill the earth and subdue it. Rule over the fish of the sea and the birds of the air and over every living creature that moves on the ground" (Genesis 1:28). With this creation mandate, the drama of human history begins.

Wolters writes:

> The meaning of history, then, must be sought against the
> background of the human management of God's work....
> What is involved here is the opening up of creation through
> the historical process. If we fail to see this, if we conceive of
> the historical differentiation that has led to such institutions as
> the school and the business enterprise, and such developments
> as urbanization and the mass media, as being basically outside
> the scope of creational reality and its responsible management
> by the human race, we will be tempted to look upon these and
> similar matters as fundamentally alien to God's purposes in
> the world and will tend to brand them as being inherently
> "secular."
>
> However, if we see that human history and the unfolding
> of culture and society are integral to creation and its develop-
> ment,... then we will be much more open to the positive

possibilities for service to God in such areas as politics and the film arts, computer technology and business administration, developmental economics and skydiving.[9]

Without question, God has given mankind a huge responsibility to administer and develop His creation intelligently, fairly, and compassionately. We see that creation is much broader than our usual Sunday school picture of Adam and Eve walking hand in hand in Eden's glade. It encompasses everything—forests, plant and animal life; cities and their people. And we see that this is a responsibility for all people, each of whom has a role to play and gifts to contribute.

The only problem is that things have not gone so well. Over the course of history, people haven't honored God or followed His principles. As the Old Testament era drew to a close, matters were in disarray. Because of His wonderful love for His people, God Himself bore the responsibility for making things right by sending His Son to earth to take on the burden of people's sins. Thus opened the time of the New Testament, as Jesus Christ stepped onto the stage in human form.

Things weren't immediately much better. Despite Christ's authoritative teaching, His many miracles, and His habit of loving the outcast and despised, many people rejected Him. Those who remained true were shattered by the revelation that He intended to die and leave them. Without the prospect of His companionship, they grew frightened and forlorn. So Christ had one more task: to teach them how to live in and respond to the world after He rejoined His Father in heaven.

Christians today are still confused about how to deal with a world in which Christ's kingdom is not fully established and won't be until He returns at the end of the age. It's crucial to understand what Christ meant us to do here in the meantime. His laws for civilization, so majestically revealed in the Old Testament, still apply in the New Testament.

Of course, we all long to be with Christ in heaven and to take along as many people as we can. But our duties in the world—that part of creation which God has entrusted to our care—haven't ceased. So we must turn to the New Testament for more instruction on how to live in this present age.

CHAPTER EIGHT

What It Means to Love the World

IF THERE IS ONE THING MOST CHRISTIANS CAN AGREE ON, it is that they shouldn't be worldly. But just what does that mean? And what is it about the world that we are to avoid? Here's where things get a bit fuzzy.

The New Testament mentions the world 176 times, but when one begins to look at all those verses, it's easy to become confused. We read in John's Gospel that God sent us His one and only Son because He so loved the world (John 3:16). But then we find in John's first letter, "Do not love the world or anything in the world. If anyone loves the world, the love of the Father is not in him" (1 John 2:15). Paul doesn't help matters much. He writes that God cared enough to reconcile the world through Christ (2 Corinthians 5:19). But can this be the same Paul who boasted about only one thing, that he had died to the world (Galatians 6:14)? And here's John again, telling us in his Gospel that Jesus didn't come to judge the world but to save it (John 12:47), seemingly in contradiction to James, who writes that any friend of the world is an enemy of God (James 4:4).

It isn't difficult to see why some people read their Bibles and plunge into the world's problems, believing that since Christ loved the world so much, they should develop a love for it as well. On the other hand, it's obvious why some Christians might read the same pages and conclude that it is ungodly even to help citizens register to vote.

What's happening here is that our English translations use *world* to mean a great number of things. It can mean the duration of our age, the cares and temptations of life, the people of the world, the created universe, secular life, material possessions, the realm of Satan, the focus of God's saving mercy, or the object of His divine judgment.[1] Two Greek words, generally, are translated as "world" in the New Testament. The first, *aion,* usually refers to an age or time, while the second, *kosmos,* commonly refers to the world's people or the whole created order. This, however, is not always the case. Each word, at times, takes on the other's meaning. The only way to understand how the word is used is to look at the context and try to decide just what the Bible is talking about. It is important to sort this out because *world* pops up so often.

THE COLD WORLD

Near the end of His ministry, Jesus calls His disciples together for a heart-to-heart talk. He tells them many things, but the one thing that stuns His friends is the news that very shortly He will be with them no longer. They find this hard to take, yet Jesus tells them there is something else they must face as well. After He has left the disciples, the hatred of the world will turn upon them, and Jesus wants them to know that the hatred is not really about them but about Him. The world will hate them because they represent Him. Jesus explains this patiently and plainly:

> If the world hates you, keep in mind that it hated me first. If
> you belonged to the world, it would love you as its own. As it
> is, you do not belong to the world, but I have chosen you out
> of the world. That is why the world hates you.... They will treat
> you this way because of my name. (John 15:18-19, 21)

From time to time, I'm contacted by people who dearly want to find a job in a Christian environment such as Focus on the Family because they're tired of the increasingly alien culture in their secular company. Workstations display the pink triangle of gay activism, indicating that the cubicle is a "safe environment" for any homosexual who feels threatened by fellow workers. And who's the threat? Many times it's the Christian colleague who has merely displayed a Christian symbol or a Bible verse—he's blamed for "discriminating" against others. In some offices today, the humble cross has once again become as offensive as it was in Christ's own day, and Christ's followers feel like outcasts in their own circle of acquaintances.

In public schools we have come a long way from the days when teacher-led prayers and Bible reading were first banned from classrooms. Today, students who want to meet on their own for an after-school Bible study often face bureaucratic delay, even though the school welcomes other kinds of extracurricular clubs. If the Christian students wish not only to meet but also to post notices of their meetings on the bulletin boards where other groups advertise, they can expect their posters to be snatched away by hostile administrators. What once would have been accepted without hesitation has now become an object of discrimination, humiliation, and rejection. Sometimes it takes lawsuits to correct the problem.

This is the kind of alienation to which Jesus is referring when He says we are not "of the world." Not only are Jesus' ways foreign to the world's system, but people who belong to the worldly system are foreign to Him. Yet Jesus doesn't for one minute want His followers to ignore the world, simply because the world hates them. We're certain of this because of what comes next.

When Jesus finished speaking to His disciples in the upper room on that melancholy day, Jesus turned His attention to His Father. He prayed a remarkable prayer, a prayer from one member of the Godhead to another.

> I have given them [Jesus' disciples] your word and the world has hated them, for they are not of the world any more than I am of the world. *My prayer is not that you take them out of the world* but that you protect them from the evil one. They are not of the world, even as I am not of it. Sanctify them by the truth; your word is truth. *As you sent me into the world, I have sent them into the world.* (John 17:14-18, emphasis added)

Notice the sudden shift in emphasis here. It begins with a very negative view of the world: "The world has hated them.... They are not of the world." That is exactly what Jesus told His disciples. But it is that very world, with its evil system, into which Christ is sending His beloved followers. Jesus prays that His Father would keep His children *in* the world, for the world is their mission field.

This unkind, unchristian worldly system is to occupy the attention and energy of Christ's followers. Yet how often do we yearn to escape to our heavenly home, to leave this travail behind and be done with it. We seem transfixed not by Christ's command to enter into the world and its problems but by Jesus' rescue of His followers at the end of the age. The best-selling Christian books of our time have been *The Late, Great Planet Earth* and the *Left Behind* series, both dealing with the doctrine of the Tribulation and the final destruction of the world. We want to escape from this world, not be engaged in it.

OUR PLACE IS IN THE WORLD—FOR NOW

Christ cares passionately about the people of this world. "I did not come to judge the world," He exclaimed, "but to save it" (John 12:47). He came to bring a great light into the world, and He does so by working through His people, who are encouraged and equipped by the Holy Spirit for the task of delivering God's message of hope. The Bible knows only engagement with the world. It knows nothing of escape, even though taking on the world invites backlash and rejection.

My wife and I began dating while we were in college. On weekends, whenever we could manage it, we loved to get off campus and out of town, away from the tedium of classes, our part-time jobs, dormitory food, and tiresome roommates. Neither of us had cars, so our opportunities for escape were rare. But on our campus there were a number of students from Deb's hometown, and from time to time we could get a ride with them, spending the weekend with Deb's parents at their home. That was our escape, and we loved it. For a brief weekend, we lived in a real house, we spoke with intelligent, down-to-earth adults, and we ate home-cooked food.

We hated Sunday nights, when we had to go back to the drudgery of the college world. But as much as we wanted to remain in Deb's town, we never did. As fed up as we were with campus life, we always returned.

Why? Because for a time that world was our destiny. It was our calling. That world was where we belonged, and we had a definite purpose in being there. Our parents had sacrificed greatly so we could fulfill their wishes for us in that world.

Suppose we had said to Deb's father on one of those Sunday nights: "We don't want to go back to college. It's not our real home, and it's very difficult for us to be there. Besides, it's only a temporary home. Your home is a real home. We want to stay here." Had we said that, we would have disappointed him greatly. He knew about the trials of college life, the pointless courses and loopy professors, because he had sent other children to college. But he knew that despite the hardships, college was where his daughter belonged, the place where his purpose for his daughter's life—a college education, which was ultimately for her good—might be realized. Deb, of course, on any of those dreary Sunday nights, couldn't see it.

As I read John 17 over and over again, I get exactly these feelings—feelings of love from a Father who consigns His children to a not very pleasant world, a world He knows will bring them pain as they accomplish His purposes there. He hurts, for He knows the hardships His children will have to face in the world. But never does He suggest that they should abandon that world, for it is the place they are meant to be—for a time. No, the Bible knows nothing of escape.

JESUS: OUR MODEL IN THE WORLD

Though many people say they want to be Christlike, they wouldn't think of immersing themselves in secular society, where Christ wants His divine light to shine. In their reading of the Bible, they do not see Christ standing up to the evil government and the decadent culture of His day. If Jesus didn't do it, why should we?

This question, John Stott says, displays a woefully inadequate understanding of the Incarnation. He writes:

> The Son of God did not stay in the safe immunity of his
> heaven. He emptied himself of his glory and humbled himself

to serve. He became little, weak and vulnerable. He entered
into our pain, our alienation and our temptations.... He had
come not to be served, he said, but to serve and to give his life
as a ransom price for the release of others.[2]

This is the model that Christ has set for us—service wherever the
need exists, in whatever forum is appropriate for our talents and person-
alities. "As the Father has sent me, I am sending you" (John 20:21).

And of course, Jesus did indeed plunge into the seamy world of sin;
He did not hide His light under a bushel. He made a point of taking
meals with tax collectors, prostitutes, and known sinners of appalling
reputation, to the extent that the Pharisees were affronted by Him. On
one particular day, when Jesus was surrounded by crowds, He spied
Zacchaeus, one of the chief tax collectors, and shouted to him that He
wanted to visit him at Zacchaeus's own home. I suspect that many people
were insulted by what Jesus did that day. Tax collectors were not much
loved by their countrymen, because they were turncoats, Jewish citizens
in the employ of the Roman occupation army. Men like Zacchaeus
extorted taxes from their neighbors for the Roman tribute, and they were
allowed to keep whatever excess taxes they could wrench for themselves.

Nor did Jesus stop simply at reaching out to individuals in need of
Him. His compassion for the common people forced Him to launch a
frontal attack on the cultural and religious authorities of His world.
Besides ignoring their rules and blasting their practices, He told them
bluntly, "Woe to you, teachers of the law and Pharisees, you hypocrites!
You travel over land and sea to win a single convert, and when he
becomes one, you make him twice as much a son of hell as you are"
(Matthew 23:15). Christ went after one of their prized institutions with
a whip, driving out of the temple everyone who was there only to make
a buck off of sincere worshipers.

He was no easier on governmental figures. Give to Caesar, He said,
only what is Caesar's. And He rebuffed a death threat from Herod, calling him a fox (Luke 13:32). Just before that, John the Baptist had also
"rebuked Herod the tetrarch because of Herodias, his brother's wife, and
all the other evil things he had done" (Luke 3:19), which got him killed.

WE'RE KNOWN BY OUR ACTIONS

Jesus' example is clear. In this present world, a life of faith must be a life of service. Evangelical Christians have the first part down well. We understand that salvation is by faith. But we are less sure about serving the world, at least when any effective attempt at it goes beyond helping individuals to address the structures and societal powers at the root of much human suffering. We ought to focus more on it, because this task of living for others is not an incidental thing. God is serious about it. John, in his first letter, puts the matter this way:

> We know that we have passed from death to life, because we love our brothers. Anyone who does not love remains in death.... This is how we know what love is: Jesus Christ laid down his life for us. And we ought to lay down our lives for our brothers. If anyone has material possessions and sees his brother in need but has no pity on him, how can the love of God be in him? Dear children, let us not love with words or tongue but with actions and in truth. (1 John 3:14, 16-18)

James puts the same issue bluntly: "Faith by itself, if it is not accompanied by action, is dead" (James 2:17). And Jesus Himself was the most blunt: "Not everyone who says to me, 'Lord, Lord,' will enter the kingdom of heaven" (Matthew 7:21).

THE PAST, PRESENT, AND FUTURE OF SALVATION

We are happy when someone gives his heart to Christ and receives the gracious reward of eternal life. Too often, however, the matter is left there. *Another sinner has been saved,* we sigh in relief. *That's that.* What an incomplete picture this is. There are really three "tenses" of salvation—past, present, and future.

The past tense of salvation is the moment we first repented of our sins and accepted Christ. We call this *justification.* But then the divine miracle continues. Like a caterpillar that transforms into a butterfly, our love for Christ should cause us to grow more obedient to Him. Obedience is the natural outworking of belief. This present tense of salvation we call *sanctification.* It is the motivation for an abundance of selfless living—a time of testing, pruning, struggling to become ever more like Christ. There can be no gold, Peter tells us, without the refiner's fire that heats it and burns away the impurities (1 Peter 1:7).

But Peter also tells us "we ain't seen nuttin' yet." This is salvation's future tense, called *glorification.* Peter writes:

> In his great mercy he has given us new birth into a living hope
> through the resurrection of Jesus Christ from the dead, and
> into an inheritance that can never perish, spoil or fade—kept in
> heaven for you, who through faith are shielded by God's power
> until the coming of the salvation that is ready to be revealed in
> the last time. (1 Peter 1:3-5)

Over the long course of history, Christians who have taken these truths seriously have been known for their compassion in times of widespread human suffering. The great campaign by William Wilberforce to abolish the British slave trade, and the persistence of those who ended slavery in our country, as we will show (see Appendix A-1), are remarkable examples of Christ's love, doubly so because the people who led them sustained such a high cost in personal rebukes, mental strain, and physical assaults.

Not surprisingly, some church leaders are embarrassed by Christians who try to address today's problems and earn only the merciless criticism of the secular news media. These leaders want Christians to back away from social engagement, to make Christianity acceptable and noncontroversial. At the very time when there should be cohesion among Christians as they face the attacks and disappointments of a fallen world, these voices send a most uncertain sound; they tell Christians it is time to disengage from the world and retreat from confrontation with evil. To these dissenters we now turn.

Part Three

PROVING THE CRITICS WRONG BY DOING IT RIGHT

CHAPTER NINE

Why Some People Shun Engagement

IN THE LATE SEVENTIES, A NEW ORGANIZATION burst upon the American political scene. It was determined to stop the cultural slide by rousing conservative Christians to take seriously their responsibilities as citizens. Called the Moral Majority, it was founded by a Baptist pastor of immense skill and deep conviction, Jerry Falwell, who had built a huge church in Lynchburg, Virginia. His new organization wanted to influence the country for righteousness. It leaped into action during the 1980 presidential campaign, and when Ronald Reagan won his surprising victory that year, the Moral Majority was given substantial credit for having brought fundamentalists into politics.

Cal Thomas, a former newsman with NBC, and Ed Dobson (no relation to Dr. James Dobson), a pastor, signed on as executives in those early days of the Moral Majority. As the 1980s unfolded, the organization found that national righteousness was a far tougher objective than anticipated. Much of its agenda lay unaccomplished, even with a conservative president in office. Although it didn't achieve its goals, the Moral Majority did awaken evangelical Christians to many evils, abortion chief among them.

But there were problems. The elite media didn't care for these religious newcomers, so the Moral Majority was criticized and ridiculed with abandon. Fund-raising appeals took on a strident tone, and the Moral Majority gained a combative, divisive reputation. In addition, their pledge to restore morality to America faltered because the mere presence of a conservative president proved not to be the panacea some had hoped for. Disillusioned by all of this, Dobson and Thomas quit.

Now the two men have turned against their former employer, as well as other Christian organizations fighting for social causes, in a book called *Blinded by Might*. The reasons for their discouragement are several. First, they say that after 20 years of Christian activism (year one being the start of the Moral Majority), the agenda has not been achieved, and it is futile to believe that government will ever be the answer to the country's moral ailments. Second, they say that Christian leaders and organizations engaged in campaigns for social reform are doing it for perverse motives (hence the book's title). Finally, they argue that because government will never be able to reform culture, the only fruitful path for the church is quiet, persistent evangelism.

As I read the book, it became obvious to me that the authors were writing primarily out of their own unsatisfying experience. For if they have a defined ethic of noninvolvement based on Scripture, they have not presented it in any detail. What are evident throughout the book are the bruises and scratches from their days in the moral briar patch. They got hurt, and they want everyone else to avoid the same fate. These men mean well to warn us all, but some of us have been in the thickets for a long time and by now are accustomed to getting scratched. The picture they present is a distorted one. The book reminds me of those old-time carnival fun house mirrors, the ones that squash and stretch body shapes into hilarious and grotesque proportions. Thomas and Dobson have done the same to the body of Christ. I find their analysis faulty in four primary ways.

FOUR OBJECTIONS

First, the book distorts the doctrine of sinful human nature. The authors contend that controversy draws people away from the gospel and that society will only be changed "one heart at a time." The book says that "morality is never activated from the top down. It is achieved from the bottom up—one person at a time, one family at a time, one street at a time, one community at a time—until the entire culture is changed—not by laws but heart by heart.... It is easier to pass a law. But laws do not change people. Trickle-down morality does not work."[1] The authors also write that justice will come only from "a radical redemption of society, which itself flows from a radical redemption of individuals. Flawed people with flawed thinking and flawed tactics cannot heal a flawed culture."[2]

As I pondered those words, I wondered what a slave in the American South might have said if he were to hear that only renewed hearts, not laws, can change society. The revival in the early 1800s known as the Second Great Awakening was the most sweeping one-heart-at-a-time spiritual transformation the American church had ever seen, but it did not directly dislodge the evil of slavery. In fact, many slave-owning Southerners were professing Christians who neatly fit slavery into their theology, and they saw no need for a change of heart. But the awakening did cause one young convert named Theodore Weld to begin agitating for a law that would force people to give up their slaves. It was this law, in the form of Abraham Lincoln's Emancipation Proclamation, that changed the slaves' lives and those of their descendants. (See Appendix A-1 for more on Weld.)

The real error here is the belief that enough people will respond to the gospel message to build a good society quietly and sweetly from within. That sentiment has become a cliché in many church circles today, but it is naive. After all, the gospel message is a message of love. The very essence of love is that it is voluntary—no one can force anyone to love anyone else, and thus people are free to reject the gospel. Sadly, many do. Most of the people who heard Jesus' message rejected Him, and most of the philosophers on Mars Hill who heard Paul preach spurned him as well.

Throughout history there has never been a thoroughly Christian society, never a time when society became good "one heart at a time." Wesley and Booth succeeded in converting many ordinary, powerless people, but each of these leaders also attracted numerous influential critics who tried to thwart them in every way possible. These Christian reformers simply ignored, outlasted, and outdebated their critics, winning begrudging acceptance only by the fruitfulness of their work.

The second problem with *Blinded by Might* is that it misinterprets the role of citizenship. The authors recognize the biblical teaching that our governing authorities "have been established by God" (Romans 13:1), and they rightly conclude that Christians should submit to and respect the government. But in Ed Dobson's words, such respect means "willingly and completely subjecting ourselves to that authority."[3] This raises a question in my mind. If God has established government, just as He has established the church, shouldn't we do what we can to be sure it functions properly, just as we do our churches? Unlike the Roman Empire in the first century, our country is a participatory republic. We have the *obligation* to make our views heard and to get involved in dialogue. Our government asks us, as citizens, to participate, not merely to shut up and obey. In the United States, "We, the people" means Christians as well as non-Christians. Submission in our political system includes being willing to contribute to the political process, not withdraw from it.

Third, the book fails to grasp the nature of biblical righteousness, opting instead for a truncated, individualistic view. Ed Dobson writes that among the requests for help that his church received was a letter from Focus on the Family (it came from me, as a matter of fact) asking for assistance with a ballot initiative that would stop casino gambling in Michigan. Because this request was "political," Dobson wouldn't get his church involved. But anyone who has studied the gambling issue knows that gambling, with its lure of quick riches, preys upon poor people. They, more than anyone, yearn to break free of their plight. Many advertising strategies for lotteries and casinos have been aimed directly at the poor. They play—and lose—larger percentages of their income than do people who are better off.

Repeatedly the Bible admonishes Christians to ensure that the poor are not oppressed, and there is no clearer example of such exploitation than legalized gambling. It is a travesty that church leaders, who have potent moral voices in their communities, fall silent on such issues of righteousness. Dobson exempts his church from all of them lest it be soiled by the "nasty business" of politics.

To those Christian leaders who do speak out on issues of righteousness, the book applies sinister motives. Cal Thomas writes:

Why do so many American Christians need to feel wanted and appreciated and see their politicians reflecting the way they pray and behave? Why do they seek validation in visibility? Is it because of some deep sense of inferiority? Is their faith so fragile that it is only in seeing it manifested in the corridors of political power in Washington that they feel justified?[4]

This is the central accusation of the book, an insinuation that those who have spoken out have not done so because of their concern for righteousness, or because of their compassion for the unborn and victimized, but because they seek to bask in political power.

Actually, those of us who have been in the middle of public policy campaigns find the experience grueling and frustrating, because sometimes so little is accomplished and the criticism from the secular world is so intense. We persist for only one reason—because it is the right thing to do. Our Lord commands it. And we take heart from Christian reformers of the past who have changed things for the better through their determination.

Fourth, because there is so much evidence that Christian people have done significant good over the years by addressing cultural problems rather than hiding from them, and because so many Bible passages do support the public role of the gospel, it is difficult for this book to make a consistent argument about why the church should isolate itself from culture. In fact, the book is logically inconsistent with itself in several places.

For example, after trying to argue that government cannot make society good, the book acknowledges that it was the U.S. Supreme Court that struck down segregation in public schools in 1954, thereby dealing a hard blow to the evil of racism. But the book explains this by saying that the justices could do what they did because they were appealing to a moral code that "deep in their hearts" Americans knew was right.

That's nonsense. Segregationists in the South opposed integration with every ounce of their strength in the 1950s and 1960s. It was federal troops and federal court orders that broke the back of school segregation, not some moral consensus of white Southerners. And this illustrates the very point that Thomas and Dobson try to deny in their book. The government can be a powerful force for good, as shown by its support of integration, or it can be a powerful force for evil, if morally minded people turn away from it in violation of Scripture.

MORE PROBLEMS

Aside from those four main blunders, the book is chock full of other problems:

Ed Dobson suggests that civil rights is one issue of righteousness on which the church should sometimes take public positions. He quotes approvingly a theologian named H. M. Kuitert, who argues that in situations in which oppressed people have no access to the political system, the church should speak for them. Dobson suggests therefore that it was appropriate for the American black church to speak out on behalf of black people against racial bias, and that the German church should have spoken on behalf of Jews during the Nazi regime.

I have two problems with such a statement. First, I cannot imagine why it would be appropriate for the black church, but not the white church, to speak against racial injustice, or why just the German church, and not all churches, should speak against the Holocaust. Surely righteousness transcends race.

Second, both of the actions that Dobson approves of are the sort that draws the church directly into national politics, which is exactly what Dobson insists the church must avoid. The black church was the nerve center of the civil rights campaigns, thoroughly enmeshed with and dependent upon the cooperation of the Eisenhower and Kennedy administrations. Furthermore, the campaign for civil rights for American black people, led mostly by black ministers, was by far more controversial and divisive than any campaign led by the Moral Majority, for which the authors are now repenting.

Cal Thomas objects to politically conservative Christians using Jesus' salt metaphor in Matthew 5:13 "as the rationalization for their political involvement." He argues, "They say that political activism is part of the 'salting,' or preserving process. But this is not entirely true, perhaps not even mainly true. Salt does its primary work when it is invisible, not when it's seen."[5] Apparently, Thomas thinks activism is always or at least primarily overt, loud, and attention-getting. That is not so. Most battles for righteousness are conducted quietly—sending a polite letter to your congressman, conveying reason and truth to fellow members of a local committee —just as you would expect from the picture of salt penetrating meat.

Sometimes the authors' inconsistencies cause them to bump heads. It is Cal Thomas who castigates public schools: "Why don't we who are church-going, value-conscious citizens see ourselves as upholding the standard of truth and bring the government school kids to our schools instead of sending our children to theirs?"[6] Yet Ed Dobson suggests just the opposite two chapters later: "Could it be that the moral and educational decline of American public schools is in part due to this exodus of people of faith? What if we shut down every Christian school in America and the students, teachers and administrators returned to the public schools—would that have a positive effect?"

In reflecting on the work of William Wilberforce, the evangelical British member of Parliament who led the successful 20-year campaign against the British slave trade, Dobson draws these conclusions: "Changing moral issues in the realm of politics takes time.... [It] takes persistence. Withdrawing from the process will ultimately spell defeat."[7] But four pages later, Thomas asserts flatly, "We will never have 'trickle-down' morality in America."[8] He uses this disparaging term to mean that government cannot do what his coauthor has just said the British Parliament did under Wilberforce's influence.

In some places the book is just baffling. A chapter titled "Focus on the Family, Not on Politics" criticizes Dr. James Dobson for, well, trying too hard, I suppose. Thomas writes: "Underneath Dr. Dobson's highly commendable zeal is a potential zealotry that is eating away at the benefits that can come with rightly applied zeal."[9] In Thomas's formulation, being zealous is good but being known as a zealot is bad. Thomas takes Dr. Dobson to task for threatening to leave the Republican Party, and encouraging as many people to leave as possible, at a time when the party was failing to abide by its own platform. The problem, according to Thomas, is that Dr. Dobson wants everything his way or he will leave. With him there is no compromise, no patience for incremental steps in public policy.

Is not the reality, however, precisely the opposite? It is Dr. Dobson who is still in the fight, still criticizing, cajoling, and encouraging politicians to do the right thing on important moral issues. It is Cal Thomas and Ed Dobson who, not achieving their Moral Majority agenda after 20 years, claim to have given up on the political process and seem to suggest that all Christians should do so as well. This is baffling in itself, for Thomas obviously hasn't given up on the political process. After he left the Moral Majority, he became a political commentator.

These writers misunderstand the role of men like James Dobson and Jerry Falwell. Although they have vastly different backgrounds, leadership styles, and strategies, Dobson and Falwell occupy prophetic roles in American society. It is their calling to declare what is right, what is absolute, and what is in accordance with God's standard of righteousness. It is their role to stand outside the political process and act as a moral force upon it. Theirs is not the same calling that leads people into political life.

Politicians inhabit a different world entirely. Theirs is a world of compromise, of halfway measures and tedious negotiations. They respond to pressure from voters because they want to remain in office. When that pressure comes from moral leaders, they feel encouraged to stand strong and compromise as little as possible.

At Focus on the Family we are constantly beseeched by conservative politicians to rouse our radio constituency on behalf of good legislation, for a flood of letters and phone calls can help their cause. The frustration felt by such people as James Dobson and Jerry Falwell is that all too frequently they—along with their colleagues who lead similar ministries—seem to be the only Christian leaders who constantly speak out. If more did, particularly pastors, the climate for moral legislation would vastly improve. But such is not the case.

BLIND CITIZENSHIP?

One of the country's best-known evangelical pastors and Bible teachers, John MacArthur, has written a book containing some of the same themes we heard from Cal Thomas and Ed Dobson. In MacArthur's way of thinking, there is little room for the everyday activities of citizenship or grassroots activism, of letting one's voice be heard. He says that "God does not call the church to influence the culture by promoting legislation.... Nor does He condone any type of radical activism that would ... seek removal of government officials we don't agree with."[10]

Instead, he seems much more comfortable with straitjacketed obedience, even to ungodly demands of corrupt government. (For example, MacArthur believes even the American Revolution was "a violation of New Testament principles, and any blessings that God has bestowed on America have come in spite of that disobedience by the Founding Fathers."[11]) He states flatly: "We are to obey *every* [author's emphasis] civil authority, no matter how immoral, cruel, ungodly or incompetent he or she might be."[12]

MacArthur makes a shocking statement about how to respond to such immorality in government. He writes, "From time to time as appropriate, we should respectfully remind our government authorities that God 'disciplines nations' (Psalm 94:10).... The founders and leaders of any good government will recognize the presence of God in the process and will not dare to exclude His principles from the conduct of governing."[13] That, apparently, is all it should take. Following this logic to its conclusion, does it also mean that if a government does not recognize godly principles, it is not a "good" government, and not being good, it is then an evil government? And if it is evil, should not Christians stand against evil?

The book levels harsh criticisms at citizens who raise their voices to elected officials. MacArthur's words to describe them are disparaging. They are engaged in "persistent lobbying" and "self-righteous confrontation." He sees them as "rabble-rousing malcontents" who take spiritual battles "into the streets" and who engage in "demonstrating, protesting, boycotting, and blockading anything that conflicts with their 'traditional values.' " He indicts Christian activists as people who are "forcing people to adopt our biblical standards of morality." He describes pro-life campaigners primarily in harsh terms: They are people who block abortion clinics and bomb them, and they are people who kill clinic workers and doctors. We should all refrain, he says, from "wasting our time ... trying to bring about moral reform."

MacArthur makes the same mistake as Cal Thomas and Ed Dobson when he says that "in the truest sense, the moral, social, and political state of a people is irrelevant to the advance of the gospel."[14] That's untrue. The two *are* connected, especially in the reverse order: The advance of the gospel often has a significant impact on the moral, social, and political state of a people. When a person becomes a Christian and applies his beliefs to what he sees, he cannot properly ignore what is wrong, because he has learned the biblical standard of what is right. The great revivals of the eighteenth and nineteenth centuries sensitized new Christians to the presence of evil, and Christian conversion brought evangelical Christian people into the front rank of the campaign against slavery (see Appendix A-1). Likewise, while the evangelical pastors of Nicaragua tried to ignore the social evils brought on by the corruption of the Somoza government in the 1970s, they could not ignore one of the gospel's most central stories—the parable of the Good Samaritan.

In the midst of his roundhouse criticism of Christian activism, MacArthur turns sharply and acknowledges that some modest level of citizen participation is appropriate "as long as we realize such interest is not vital to our spiritual growth, our righteous testimony or the advancement of the kingdom of Christ."[15] In other words, we can do it as long as we understand that it isn't worth much.

This is a curious thing, this sudden reversal of course, the begrudging acknowledgment that some societal involvement is appropriate for Christians. The Thomas/Dobson book acknowledges the same, after spending many pages criticizing Christians who are active. It seems even these authors cannot wholly deny the need for such involvement. As Stephen Mitchell, the noted Yale law professor and author of *The Culture of Disbelief,* observed:

> Many early architects of the conservative political coalition sometimes described as the Religious Right, depressed by the nation's shoulder-shrugging reaction to the Monica Lewinsky scandal, have changed their minds and returned to the eighteenth-century Christian ideal, urging evangelicals to disengage from the culture generally and, in particular, to stay away from politics.

For most religious believers, however, disengagement is not an option. Those who think their only task is to prepare themselves and their families for the next world nevertheless often discover that they must engage with this world in order to obtain the cultural space for their preparation. Politics, often, will be one of the tools for preserving the space. And religionists who believe they have an obligation to engage the culture in order to work for the betterment of God's creation will presumably continue to do just that. Religion, in short, will be in politics. It cannot reasonably be kept out.[16]

I think these men, Cal Thomas, Ed Dobson, and John MacArthur, all learned and experienced people, do want to see Christians engage the world. But like the rest of us, they long to see it done intelligently and compassionately. And more than anything, they do not want to see social involvement harm opportunities for the spread of the gospel. They are rightly concerned that evangelism will suffer, both from negative coverage in the media and from the ferocity of response in some corners of the secular world, whenever Christians stake out moral claims in public. I sense a yearning in the pages of these books for Christians always to work on these moral issues in an unobtrusive way so that few feathers are ruffled.

But I don't think it's possible. Ultimately, it is not the style of our Christian arguments that creates the problem (though our approach *does* matter—see chapter 10); it is the very *existence* of those arguments that brings on the attacks. No matter how lovingly we state what we have to say, the fact that we want to be part of the debate at all produces animosity in our opponents.

Secularists would dearly love to see Christianity stay safely tucked away behind the four walls of the church. But that cannot be. Jesus presents us with a bold challenge when He invites us to be His followers. In the same sermon in which He shifted the task of righteousness to center stage, He called us to something else, something very public. He commanded us to be salt and light in society. When He did that, He forever precluded the notion that Christianity, properly lived, would be uncontroversial.

We must be careful, however, not to stir up *needless* antagonism. We are advised by the apostle Paul, "If it is possible, as far as it depends on you, live at peace with everyone" (Romans 12:18). Next, we consider how to do that.

CHAPTER TEN

Is Activism Always Ugly?

I HAD JUST ARRIVED AT WORK THAT MORNING WHEN IRV, my city editor, came rushing over with a story off the Associated Press wire. It was only half past seven, and already Irv's shirttail was loose and his hair askew. That was Irv.

"It's from the federal court and it might have an effect on churches here. Get me some local comment, and I want it for the first edition."

"Well, and a 'good morning' to you, too, Irving," I muttered as I reached for the phone book. I knew little about local churches, and I was new on the job as a reporter for the *Rochester Times-Union*, which meant anybody could throw me anything. We didn't have an official religion reporter at the time, mostly because no one wanted the job. Religion wasn't familiar terrain for many of us in the newsroom.

The phone directory listed a local affiliate for the National Council of Churches. *Hmm.* That sounded official. I called, reading the story to myself while the phone rang at the other end. A man answered and identified himself as the executive director. He said the council represented a broad cross section of Protestant churches in the area, and he'd be glad to comment on the federal court ruling. I took down some quotes, included the background from the wire story, and filed the story. It ran that afternoon.

The next day Irv came sailing over to my desk again, this time waving a phone message. A Baptist pastor was angry with my story. "Better call him," said Irv, glaring at me. City editors are so helpful. I called the minister, and Irv was right. The man was angry indeed. He accused the paper of slanted news coverage for getting only the liberal view of the previous day's court story, and he wanted to know why we didn't care what the Bible-believing churches had to say. I had no clue what the man was talking about. I probably would have asked him to slow down and elaborate, but he made me mad. He was accusing me of bias when in fact I wasn't biased at all, just ignorant. I suggested he write a letter to the editor, and I ended the conversation.

That was nearly 30 years ago. Honestly, I cannot remember what the court issue was about, but I can recall the anger in that minister's voice. I remember thinking that I wanted nothing to do with the Bible-believing churches, whatever they were.

We must learn *how* to engage the broader culture, *how* to approach people whose views are sharply different from our own, whose need for Jesus is apparent and who regard our presence with something less than enthusiasm. The New Testament calls us to be people of character. Regardless of what we do, what career we embark on, what prayers God answers or doesn't answer, Christ wants us to become like Himself in every aspect of our lives. The rough times that Jesus permits to enter our lives give us plenty of opportunities to monitor our progress. People who understand this, and who strive to conform their own character to Christ's, will become leaders. For they will know how to respond to the daily crises that throw many other people into turmoil. More important, those who strive to take on the character of Christ will draw people to themselves, for everyone will want to be around them.

CHRISTIAN CHARACTER SUITS LEADERS

The apostle Paul spoke directly about how we should live, given the freedom we have and the opportunities that life affords us. Here is what he says in Galatians, according to *The Message,* a contemporary paraphrase:

> It is obvious what kind of life develops out of trying to get
> your own way all the time: repetitive, loveless, cheap sex; a
> stinking accumulation of mental and emotional garbage; fren-
> zied and joyless grabs for happiness; …cutthroat competition;

all-consuming-yet-never-satisfied wants; a brutal temper; an impotence to love or be loved; divided homes and divided lives; small-minded and lopsided pursuits; the vicious habit of depersonalizing everyone into a rival; uncontrolled and uncontrollable addictions; ugly parodies of community. I could go on.

This isn't the first time I have warned you, you know. If you use your freedom this way, you will not inherit God's kingdom.

But what happens when we live God's way? He brings gifts into our lives, much the same way that fruit appears in an orchard—things like affection for others, exuberance about life, serenity. We develop a willingness to stick with things, a sense of compassion in the heart, and a conviction that a basic holiness permeates things and people. We find ourselves involved in loyal commitments, not needing to force our way in life, able to marshal and direct our energies wisely.[1]

Who wouldn't be attracted to a person exhibiting character traits such as those in the last paragraph! This is the "fruit of the Spirit," the Christian graces of love, joy, peace patience, kindness, goodness, faithfulness, gentleness, and self-control. By prayer, by practice, and by devotion to God's Word, we can begin to make these traits our own.

Sometimes that word *gentleness* is translated as "meekness," and in our culture a meek person is a pussycat—a pushover. Meekness is not a trait to which many people aspire. But this is not what the word means. It has to do with the settled acceptance of God's dealings toward us, and with judging our circumstances to be the ones that God has permitted, whether for good or ill.[2]

Biblically speaking, meekness can include the expression of anger, provided the anger is rightly directed. Jesus described Himself as "gentle [or meek] and humble in heart" (Matthew 11:29), and Paul described Christ as a man of "meekness and gentleness" (2 Corinthians 10:1). Yet Jesus' anger rose when a group of Jews, looking for reasons to accuse Him, sat expectantly in the synagogue as Jesus was about to heal a man on the Sabbath. Their legalism affronted Jesus. "He looked around at them in anger and, deeply distressed at their stubborn hearts, said to the man, 'Stretch out your hand.' He stretched it out, and his hand was completely restored" (Mark 3:5).

Likewise, when Jesus entered the temple and found that it had been turned into a commercial extravaganza, He was deeply agitated. Fashioning a whip from cords, He physically drove the money changers from the temple. Obviously, then, a meek person has strength and determination to act, but for the right reasons and at the right times. Meekness is strength under control.

Elsewhere, Paul advises Christians to "clothe yourselves with compassion, kindness, humility, gentleness [meekness] and patience" (Colossians 3:12). And when Peter wrote to the persecuted Christians scattered throughout Asia Minor, he bore in on one of those traits, humility: "All of you, clothe yourselves with humility toward one another, because, 'God opposes the proud but gives grace to the humble.' Humble yourselves, therefore, under God's mighty hand, that he may lift you up in due time" (1 Peter 5:5-6).

Paul and Peter used the same metaphor to describe how these virtues apply. Their admonition was to "clothe yourselves" in them. Clothing is not natural to human beings. It is, quite literally, a put-on. But all of us, after much experience with clothing, have become accustomed to it. That is exactly how it is with these valuable character traits. If they don't seem natural, put them on anyway and cover up what comes natural. If pride is your problem, then slip on a suit of humility. You'll get used to it. If unwarranted anger has become a habit, then button on meekness and don't take it off. It will scratch, it will chafe, it will be hot and bulky. But sooner or later, it will become part of you.

THE LONG CAMPAIGN OF WILLIAM WILBERFORCE

In the bleakest of times, in the darkest of circumstances, these traits serve well those who learn to lean on them. One who did was an Englishman named William Wilberforce, an odd-looking, near-sighted runt of a man who was born to wealth and destined to a playboy's pleasure—dancing, drinking, and gambling. As a counterweight to his physical shortcomings, Wilberforce also possessed a gift for speaking, a fine intellect, and a gregarious personality. His assets were those of a promising politician, and indeed he won a seat in Parliament in 1780.

One of Wilberforce's old teachers, Isaac Milner, saw greatness in him and fastened his attention on the young gadabout. Milner, a devoted Christian, counseled him to take his faith much more seriously. Milner's rigorous intellect whittled away at Wilberforce's doubts. Then Wilberforce sought further advice from another acquaintance, a celebrated minister named John Newton, whose own Christian conversion had led him away from the dissolute life of a slave ship captain. Newton, author of the words to the hymn "Amazing Grace," was a spiritually scarred veteran of many bouts with the devil, and he erased Wilberforce's last hesitations.

After his turn to faith, Wilberforce lost his zeal for the pursuit of pleasure and developed a more sober-minded focus on his work. He began treating his political adversaries more gently, and he softened his biting wit. His socialite mother feared that her son had become one of Wesley's "enthusiasts," speculating to a friend that William might actually have gone mad. The friend, more perceptive, realized the potential power in a politician of Wilberforce's natural talents when fired by zealous Christian faith. "If this is madness," the friend replied, "I hope that he will bite us all."[3]

What he bit into was an evil that would consume most of his political career: the entrenched British slave trade. In 1562, the first boatload of Africans had been captured by a British sea captain and sold in the West Indies. Since then this traffic in human misery had made British shippers and planters rich, turning sleepy British ports into boomtowns. More than 200 hundred years later, when Wilberforce stepped into public life, some 50,000 slaves a year—men, women, and children—were being captured, hideously packed like so much firewood into the bowels of ships, and hauled to the Caribbean and American colonies. The immense profits, despite death rates as high as 25 percent during the punishing sea voyages, made the British slavers and shippers an indisputable economic and political power in Britain, untouchable by any reform-minded politician.

The Traits of a Political Reformer

Wilberforce had long been troubled by the slave trade, and he was not alone. For decades the Quakers in his country had been trying to raise consciences against it, and slowly their concern had begun to spread. In 1787, members of this sect and other Christian friends of Wilberforce formed the Committee for the Abolition of the Slave Trade. He agreed to champion their cause. But was he capable? Could he and his small group of abolitionist colleagues in the House of Commons actually hope to batter down this entrenched institution of English life? The task was beyond formidable. One of Wilberforce's biographers describes the political skills that would be necessary for the gladiator who would dare wrestle this behemoth in its lair, the clubby gentility of Parliament:

> He must possess, in the first place, the virtues of a fanatic without his vices. He must be palpably single-minded and unself-seeking. He must be strong enough to face opposition and ridicule, staunch enough to endure obstruction and delay. In season and out of season, he must thrust his cause on Parliament's attention. Yet, somehow or other, Parliament must not be bored. He must not be regarded—and the planters, no doubt, would do their best to cultivate this idea—as the tiresome victim of an *idée fixe*, well-meaning, possibly, but an intolerable nuisance. Somehow or other he must be persistent, yet not unpopular.
>
> Secondly he must possess the intellectual power to grasp an intricate subject, the clarity of mind to deal with a great mass of detailed evidence, the eloquence to expound it lucidly and effectively. He must be able to speak from the same brief a score of times without surfeiting his audience with a hash of stale meat. And, since the slave trade is his theme, he must have a certain natural delicacy of feeling. He will have terrible things to say; they will form an essential part of his case; but in the choice of them and in the manner in which he says them he must avoid the besetting sin of the professional humanitarian—

he must never be morbid. He must not seem to take pleasure in dwelling on the unsavory vices of his fellow men. He must not pile up the horrors and revel in atrocious details. He must shock, but not nauseate, the imagination of his hearers.

Finally, he must be a man of recognized position in society and politics. It must be impossible for wealthy West Indians to deride him in London drawing rooms as an obscure crank, a wild man from beyond the pale.[4]

If this was Wilberforce's job description, he filled it exceptionally well. He began introducing and debating his slave trade bills year by year, starting in 1787, and year by year they were defeated. But his winsomeness, rounded and deepened by his Christian commitment, warmed some of his implacable foes, and he would not be flustered by the fulminations of others. His conviction that abolition was righteous before God and inevitable in a free society kept him and his colleagues soldiering ahead, year after tedious year. Two years into the campaign, he received an insightful letter from the aged crusader John Wesley, written just a week before the preacher's death.

"Unless the divine power has raised you up," the old crusader wrote, "to be as *Athanasius contra mundum,* I see not how you can go through your glorious enterprise.... Unless God has raised you up for this very thing, you will be worn out by the opposition of men and devils; but if God be for you, who can be against you?... Go on, in the name of God and in the power of His might, till even American slavery (the vilest that ever saw the sun) shall vanish away before it."[5] Writing in his own spiritual diary shortly after, Wilberforce reflected on the true source of his energies: "May I look to Him for wisdom and strength and the power of persuasion ... and ascribe to Him all the praise if I succeed, and if I fail, say from the heart 'Thy will be done.' "[6]

In debates he was always prepared with facts and fresh illustrations to support his rhetoric, which could grow fervent but never harsh. His associates on the committee for abolition toiled unendingly to bring new data to him. They prowled docksides and taverns to collect firsthand anecdotes from slaving crews. They crawled through the reeking underdecks of slave ships riding at anchor in order to measure for themselves the dimensions of those squalid holds for human cargo. They purchased shackles, thumbscrews, and torture instruments to prove the inhumanity of the trade, and always they searched and searched for more.

Eventually it was his opponents' arguments that grew tiresome. The slave bloc in Parliament maintained that abolition would ruin the economy of English ports as well as the colonies; that blacks were happier on "Christian" plantations after their rescue from heathen darkness; that abolition might bring the West Indies to declare independence from Britain; and that without the British in the business, France or Spain might seize the trade and profit from it. Gradually the weight of it all began to shrivel under the withering force of Wilberforce's facts, the undeniable humanity of his cause, and the unceasing gentility of his manner. Year by year the abolition bloc in Parliament grew. Finally, in 1807, 20 years after Wilberforce had introduced his first bill, it gained a majority, and the slave trade was prohibited. On that happy occasion, Wilberforce—winsome as ever—turned to one of his beloved colleagues, Henry Thornton, and said, "Well, Henry, what shall we abolish next?"

William Wilberforce exemplifies the power of Christian graces to overcome tremendous obstacles in national affairs. He believed simply that his cause was godly, and therefore just. For that reason he wouldn't give it up. His desire to emulate Christ in all his actions attracted people to him while it also whittled down the sharp edges of his opponents. His career testifies to the accomplishments that are possible when Christians who are properly prepared, and properly motivated, enter public life.

LIVING THE LIFE OF ROMANS 12

The apostle Paul has advice that is especially appropriate for people in public life, or who think they want to enter it, because his words help one maintain equilibrium in the face of bitter disappointment and deep frustration. While these trials at times befall all of us, they are the daily torment of any who seek to accomplish good in hostile circumstances by persuading, debating, and building relationships.

Love must be sincere. Hate what is evil; cling to what is good.
Be devoted to one another in brotherly love. Honor one
another above yourselves. Never be lacking in zeal, but keep
your spiritual fervor, serving the Lord. Be joyful in hope,
patient in affliction, faithful in prayer. Share with God's people
who are in need. Practice hospitality. Bless those who persecute
you; bless and do not curse. Rejoice with those who rejoice;
mourn with those who mourn. Live in harmony with one
another. Do not be proud, but be willing to associate with
people of low position. Do not be conceited. Do not repay
anyone evil for evil. Be careful to do what is right in the eyes of
everybody. If it is possible, as far as it depends on you, live at
peace with everyone. Do not take revenge, my friends, but
leave room for God's wrath. (Romans 12:9-19)

There is no gloominess in Paul's picture. He's telling us to wade hip-
deep into life, take it as it comes, expect the best in people, be realistic
about human nature, and keep a heavenly perspective.

We must have appreciation for people, particularly those who despise
us, because all of them matter so much to God and because we are to be
living lives of gratitude to God for His mercies to us. John puts it simply:
"We love because he first loved us" (1 John 4:19). In fact, we should be
the kind of people who draw others to ourselves. This is the attitude of
gratitude so beautifully expressed in Romans 12 and so ably lived out in
the life of William Wilberforce.

CHRISTIAN BEHAVIOR DRAWS PEOPLE

I have observed these godly characteristics in play from time to time in
public affairs, and I see how powerful they can be.

One of the more contentious issues ever to face the U.S. Congress
was the impeachment of President Clinton. In the House of Representatives, the sharpest battle of will and nerves occurred in the House Judiciary Committee. If the articles of impeachment against the president

were to advance, they first had to clear this committee, which included some of the sharpest and most ideological minds in the House.

The chairman of the committee was Henry Hyde, a Roman Catholic Republican from the suburbs of Chicago. Day after day, the committee debate over President Clinton's dishonorable activities ground on, and day after day the fiercely partisan Democrats, allies of the president, sought to delay, destroy, or discredit the impeachment bill. Republicans on the committee were equally determined to get it through the Judiciary Committee.

Throughout the ordeal, Henry Hyde was the picture of cordiality and weary patience. He never lost his temper, nor did he speak ill of his fiercest antagonists, though they sorely tried him. He maneuvered skillfully and was eminently fair with opponents, even in the teeth of their gnashing outbursts. Through it all, he even maintained the arcane language of congressional decorum.

"For what purpose does the gentle lady from California seek recognition?" Hyde asked politely, time and again, day after day, knowing full well that Rep. Maxine Waters, a ferociously partisan Democrat, was about to skewer him one more time. She was seldom a "gentle lady," but Hyde never failed to pay her the respect due her position.

In the end, Hyde's skill and patience took the fight out of the Judiciary Committee Democrats, and it passed the impeachment bill. This happened, remarkably, in the weeks following the November 1998 elections, when the Republican losses in the House were widely interpreted to mean that the Republicans should drop the unpopular issue of impeachment.

There is something else about Henry Hyde that makes his success remarkable. For many years he has been the standard bearer in the House on the most contentious issue that perennially confronts its members, the issue of abortion. While the Supreme Court has nearly tied the hands of pro-life congressmen, they do what they can to thwart abortions by insisting that no federal dollars be used to pay for them. The device by which they do this is called the Hyde Amendment, and it is the focus of partisan debate whenever it is introduced. By rights, with his implacable view against abortion, Hyde should have been written off as an ideologue, an extremist. Every scornful name applied to social conservatives should have been cast upon him.

Remarkably, this hasn't happened. In fact, Hyde has been praised by his foes. "A partisan Republican he is, but Henry is also a statesman," said Kate Michelman, the prominent leader of the National Abortion and Reproductive Rights Action League. The *New York Times*, never friendly to the pro-life movement, writes that "the silver-haired, golden-tongued law-maker has alternately frustrated, infuriated and trumped his peers with his ideological ferocity. But he has also earned their universal respect."[7]

How has he done this? How has Henry Hyde managed to earn the respect of implacable foes on the most divisive issue of the day? How did he hold to his course under the onslaught of furious opposition to the impeachment bill, so that the bilious gas of partisanship was harmlessly expelled? I asked him once, at a breakfast meeting a colleague and I had with him.

"I just try to treat everybody with respect," he said, shrugging his shoulders and turning back to his plate with an air that telegraphed, *There is nothing complicated, nothing profound here.*

Except that it *is* profound. To treat people with respect, especially people with whom one viscerally disagrees on a matter of abiding impor-tance, and to act toward them this way day after day, in the most dis-tressing of circumstances, is no small accomplishment. It is not human nature to do this. But it is commanded in the New Testament.

Not every politician who treats people kindly is a godly politician, of course. But the kind treatment of people is a godly trait, and many people find such traits to be useful, whether or not they honor the source of those virtues. The reason for this is simple. In most situations, when you display these characteristics, people are more apt to like you. If someone likes you, he's more likely to believe what you say or to respect what you stand for.

Another modern-day example of Christlike love is that of Phil Burress, a businessman who for many years has successfully led a continuing fight against pornography in Cincinnati while acting compassionately toward his foes. Burress says, "If anyone should be flying the flag of love higher, it should be we Christians. I will not let people hang the label of 'hate monger' on me. If they believe that about me, I will seek them out because I want them to get to know me personally." (Read Burress's story in Appendix A-3.)

THE REWARDS OF RELATIONSHIPS

A number of years ago, some leaders of the local Republican party in my town were unhappy about the growing number of social conservatives, mostly evangelical Christians, joining the party and becoming active. Their gripe about us was that we had "litmus tests" on issues, and they feared that anyone who didn't measure up to our beliefs would be run out. In other words, we were divisive, and therefore we wouldn't make trusted party members. Since I was one of the targets of the criticism, I responded by becoming even more active. I ran for election as vice chairman of the county organization, and I won. (Surprisingly, nobody else entered the race until the very end. Our critics turned out to be better at muttering than organizing.)

All three officers who won were social conservatives, although we didn't all share the same religious beliefs. We did share one goal; namely, we wanted to work with everybody, especially those who disagreed with our views on issues. The main project I took on was training precinct-level party workers on how to organize our party's neighborhood caucuses and walk precincts in order to get out the vote for our candidates in the fall. We decided to produce a training video—something the county organization had never before done.

The video was shot at my house by a professional producer (another of those pesky, divisive religious people) who donated most of his time to the project. We carefully selected the people to appear in the video, making sure we had both the old-timers and the newcomers represented. With the video completed, I crisscrossed the county, holding training meetings in various neighborhoods. The fall election was also a success. Our party elected the first Republican governor in our state in 28 years, and the results in our county figured prominently in that victory. All in all, it was a lot of hard work but a wonderful experience. By the end of our two-year tenure, complaints about the divisive new people in the party had disappeared.

A couple of years later, the election cycle came around again. Because it was 2000, a presidential election year, it was time to elect delegates to our national party convention. I received a telephone call from a friend who wanted to be one of those delegates, and he asked if I would support him. I was surprised that he called me, because although we had both worked hard together on party activities, I had not known him to support the pro-life plank in the national Republican platform. Therefore, my support of him as a delegate was impossible. He went on to say that since we had come to know each other, I had exerted a lot of influence on him, and he had grown to accept the pro-life position. He pledged that as a delegate to the national convention he would support the pro-life plank.

I was pleased to hear that, and I supported him as a delegate. No one deserved more the honor of representing our area at the national convention, because he was one of our party's most diligent volunteers. But I was surprised to hear him say how much I had influenced him. We had always been so busy with get-out-the-vote issues that we hadn't talked much about abortion. I think it was more my willingness to work and my kind treatment of people that had persuaded him.

I have often wondered about the woman whom the Pharisees cast before Christ in the temple courts one day, the woman caught in adultery. According to Mosaic law, she should have been killed for her sin. Indeed, her accusers were there to see to her stoning, until Christ dispatched them, and He and the woman stood alone. Noting that no one remained to condemn her, Christ said, "Then neither do I condemn you.... Go now and leave your life of sin" (John 8:11).

I wonder whether she did indeed leave her life of sin, and if so, why. Was it because of Christ's admonition to sin no more, or was it His gentle tone and lack of a condemning attitude? My guess is that she did take the straight path after hearing not only what Christ said but also the way in which He said it. His bearing was as godly as were His words.

We Christians have some tough things to say to people about their eternal destiny without Christ and about the harm they bring to themselves by immoral activities. How we say what we have to say is as important as the words we choose. That is why the Bible talks so much about the airs, the attitudes, and the actions in which our rather stark message is to be framed.

Being Christian Even in Rejection

It is especially important to maintain our Romans 12 attitudes when our words are rejected and our motives criticized. In his fight for the abolition of American slavery, Theodore Weld always employed a firm yet gentle manner when resisting the mobs. He could do this in part because he had such a strong grasp of the facts to support his cause. Those not so well prepared as he found it natural to lash out against their opponents. As it says in Ecclesiastes 10:10, "If the axe is dull and its edge unsharpened, more strength is needed." (Read more about Theodore Weld in Appendix A-1.)

Weld's charitable approach has been characteristic of reformers who have made headway against the worldly currents of their day. It was especially true of John Wesley as he sought to revive the Anglican church and enlist it in his great campaigns to rid England of rampant drunkenness, sexual debauchery, child labor, atrocities to prisoners, and clergy immorality.

Social problems like these do not readily accommodate a crusader like Wesley, whose sermons exposed those who were profiting from institutionalized sin. Established clergy disliked him as well, for he railed at the complacency of the church in the face of great evil. And so it was that Wesley was often physically assaulted, as we saw in chapter three. Here is his own account of one of his preaching experiences:

> In the evening, as I was preaching at St. Ives, Satan began to fight for his kingdom. The mob of the town burst into the room and created much disturbance; roaring and striking those that stood in the way, as though Legion himself possessed them. I would fain have persuaded our people to stand still; but the zeal of some and the fear of others, had no ears; so that finding the uproar increase [*sic*] I went into the midst, and brought the head of the mob up with me to the desk. I received but one blow to the side of the head, after which we reasoned the case, till he grew milder and milder, and at length undertook to quiet his companions.[8]

Today it is difficult to imagine that scene. Wesley steered the leader of the rabble to his pulpit, suffered a blow to the head from the man, and then, without retaliating, began to reason with him. What an example for those wanting to enter the arena of moral debate today! One historian says of him:

> Wesley, the evangelist, was a man possessed of amazing grace. Never did he lose his temper; and always was he prepared to endure a blow, if the dealing of it would relieve the hysteria of his assailant. Repeatedly, when struck by a stone or cudgel, he quietly wiped away the blood and went on preaching without so much as a frown on his face. He loved his enemies; and do what they would, they could not make him discourteous or angry. It is no exaggeration to say that Wesley instilled into the British people, a new and highly Christian conception of bravery and courage.... In danger, Wesley had taught his followers to think of the Christ before Pilate, of the Son of God before a raging, crucifying mob. Thus it was, that Wesley's serenity first broke, and later won, the heart of many a mob leader and ruthless enemy. Thus it was too that many a one-time brute came to be transformed into a gentle, saintly, class-leader and understanding shepherd of souls. This miraculous grace was the power which finally conquered the 18th-century mob.... It was not courage alone that saved Wesley. He was preserved by a tranquil dignity, by cool, steady and courteous behavior, by the entire absence of malice and anger; but above all, by those peculiar graces and powers which accompany a man of God.[9]

CROSSING BARRIERS OF HOSTILITY

Wesley's example shows us that effective Christian words must be accompanied by authentic Christian behavior if Christ's case is to be made. It worked for Wesley then and it still works today.

I'll never forget the most hostile audience I ever spoke to. It was composed of left-wing radicals, lesbian activists, and Communists. Now, it isn't difficult to find the first two in audiences these days, but there aren't many places where one can find the third group. Here we did. This audience was in a small town about 50 miles north of Beijing, China. I and three colleagues from Focus on the Family went there to participate in the United Nations Conference on Women in 1995. We decided to go because it looked as though that conference was overrun with antifamily propagandists, and we wanted to strike what blow we could for traditional values.

Prior to the start of the conference itself, there was a two-week schedule of workshops on topics of all sorts, all of them supposed to be pertinent to women from around the world. We were shocked when we read the lineup. Some of them were perfunctory and useful, but others dealt with lesbian sex techniques, worship of a female earth goddess, and strategies for distributing condoms to schoolchildren back home. Now, if you think this is a strange agenda for a United Nations event, then you haven't been keeping up with that unwieldy organization, which in recent years has become a playground for the far-out Left.

Although the conference was held in Beijing, the workshops were suddenly relocated to this remote town just before they were to commence. We suspect that the Chinese government realized what subjects were to be discussed and didn't want to taint their own people with the sort of propaganda that the leftists were about to spread around. Although the feminists squawked at being banished, the Chinese held firm.

The subject of our workshop was the value of raising children in a home headed by a man and woman joined together in marriage. Ours certainly stood out from the others, and I had no idea what kind of reception our team would receive. Many of the workshops were to be held in flimsy tentlike structures, and some were located in the skeleton of a still-unfinished building. The rain was fierce the entire time, and some of the workshops were literally washed out.

To our relief, our workshop was scheduled for a large classroom in a school building. On the morning we were to make our presentation, the room was packed. I was nervous, but at least everyone was dry and comfortable. We recognized some of the women in the audience as feminist and lesbian leaders, and we were surprised to see a group of Chinese women as well, all of them wearing Communist Party pins. We hadn't seen any Chinese participants elsewhere in the conference.

We huddled, said a prayer, and plunged in. But our first presenter didn't stick to the script. Speaking in a very gentle, friendly tone, she said, "Good morning. My name is Danielle Madison. Let's face it. Most of you are here because you hate men. Isn't that right?" (Stony silence from the audience. Finally, a few nods here and there. Whatever they expected to hear, this wasn't it.)

Danielle, again in a kind voice: "I suspect that many of you have very good reasons to hate men. Isn't that right?" (More nods this time, from all around the room. Hey, maybe this was a *sister!*)

"Let me tell you my story." And then Danielle delved into her own background, describing difficult and troubling circumstances that she had endured because of men's mistreatment of her many years earlier. The audience was warming to her. There were nods and encouraging expressions throughout the room. (I, however, was shocked. I had no idea she intended to go into all of this.)

Then she said, "Let me tell you why I am standing up here and not sitting where you are. I finally met a good man, a man named Jesus Christ. Let me tell you who He is and how He changed my life." And with that she gave a warm, wonderful testimony of her adoption into the family of God. The audience listened respectfully until she finished and sat down.

I was amazed. But it was my turn to speak. I was to present summaries of the many academic studies showing that children do best in homes with committed fathers and mothers. There are many single moms and dads whose children turn out well, I said, but statistically the best chance for those kids is in a traditional home. We had translated our material into the five official United Nations languages, and copies were available on a side table. I pointed this out and then opened the floor for questions.

It was a spirited session. They challenged us on many points, but the audience was respectful and the debate thorough. Finally, near the end of the workshop, one of the Communist Party members stood up and asked, "How can we keep our husbands from cheating on us?"

Wow! No matter what the culture or the philosophy, human hearts long for the same thing—love that will not fail. I was so surprised by the question that I can't remember what I mumbled back. I'm afraid I wasn't nearly as bold as I should have been.

Then the workshop was done. We thanked the audience, and the women in that room did something I never expected. They clapped. It wasn't resounding, but it was real, and we were moved. Ever since, I've been convinced that Christian graces can surmount the barriers of human hostility as nothing else can, leaving openings for the gospel that are unimaginable and thoroughly exciting.

Armed with Christlike character, we can do almost anything. But how does each of us decide where to direct our energy? The campaign for righteousness is being waged on a thousand fronts. Where do you and I belong? That is the subject of the final chapter.

CHAPTER ELEVEN

I'm Only One Person—
What Can I Do?

PEOPLE ARE DRAWN TO CERTAIN ISSUES for a variety of reasons. Circumstances, perhaps. A breath of the Holy Spirit. Formal study. A sudden experience that shatters apathy. For me, I was seared by the images I saw projected on the screens in the hearing rooms of the pornography commission and by testimonies like that of the 16-year-old girl whom two neighbors had molested.

Is it proper for a Christian to rage against a thing like this? Certainly it is. It is not only proper to be disturbed about what must disturb God, but in fact He desires it. The book of Hebrews contains an insightful passage about the call to righteousness. It says that those whose hearts are tugged by some violation of God's righteousness, who are moved to do what they can to restore some corner of the Kingdom, are people of maturity. Whereas Christians who don't do so are spiritual infants, still playing around with basic building blocks of the faith.

The author expresses his frustration at believers who have not advanced beyond elementary things:

> Though by this time you ought to be teachers, you need some-
> one to teach you the elementary truths of God's word all over
> again. You need milk, not solid food! Anyone who lives on
> milk, being still an infant, is not acquainted with the teaching
> about righteousness. But solid food is for the mature, who by

constant use have trained themselves to distinguish good from evil. (Hebrews 5:12-14)

Milk may be good, but milk is basic. Most people can drink milk all their lives, but all people need much more than milk if they are to grow to maturity. John Calvin put it this way: "As in building, one must never leave the foundation; yet to be always laboring in laying it would be ridiculous."[1]

In the next few verses of Hebrews we learn what this "milk" is. It is elementary teaching about faith in God, the person of Christ, repentance from sin, baptism, laying on of hands, resurrection, and judgment (Hebrews 6:1-2). In other words, it is those spiritual matters to which many churches devote most of their time. This is unfortunate, because although baby Christians must have this milk, mature Christians should be able to digest much more. They should learn about the world and determine how to respond to its transgressions of God's righteousness. This solid food is what Hebrews calls the "teaching about righteousness." It is, according to Jesus, what we should hunger and thirst after.

Every day, in every walk of life, we have choices to make about whether to approach life's problems God's way—the way of righteousness—or the world's way. Mature Christians are people who choose God's way, and who do so as second nature because they hunger and thirst to see God's way infuse every corner of their lives and every part of the world. Sometimes community leaders who are Christians, be they average people, public officeholders, pastors, or business and professional leaders, have powerful opportunities to inject God's righteousness in their spheres of influence. But they do not, for fear of offending people or of somehow being inappropriate.

William Barclay asks how someone can be said to hunger and thirst for something if he is afraid to grasp it wherever it can be found. Can a church congregation be said to hunger and thirst for righteousness if it confines its life to what happens in the sanctuary and Sunday school rooms one day a week? If a business leader allows God to influence his personal life but wouldn't think of standing for godly virtues in his corporation, can he really be hungering and thirsting for righteousness?

When someone like me, then, smolders at the perversion called pornography, I believe I am within the scope of righteousness. I conclude that I have not stunted my Christian life by laying again the foundation of Christian belief, but I have become sensitive to a transgression of righteousness that causes God's own heart to bleed. My response to this issue demonstrates that I have moved beyond the elementary milk of the Christian life.

How to Know What to Tackle

The problem here is that righteousness is a very broad objective. In fact, it encompasses everything that makes up the opposite of wickedness. Paul admonishes believers, "Do not be yoked together with unbelievers. For what do righteousness and wickedness have in common?" (2 Corinthians 6:14). Elsewhere, Jesus is praised because He has "loved righteousness and hated wickedness" (Hebrews 1:9). This means that Christians are to be sensitive to whatever evil asserts itself in the world, because those things, whether personal tragedies, catastrophic events, destructive philosophies, evil in entertainment, or wickedness in church and public life, all stand against righteousness, which mature Christians are to love.

So what am I supposed to do? Seethe at everything wrong? If that's the case, I would have burned out a long time ago. Quite obviously, with so much going wrong in society today, and with all the other relationships and responsibilities to be tended to—spiritual growth, family, church activities, job—there is limited time to focus on anything outside of one's immediate sphere. How is it possible to do this?

It is foolish to expect everyone to pay attention to every assault on God's standard of righteousness. He naturally sensitizes different people to different things, and He calls people or organizations to a variety of roles, as a result of the burden He has planted within them. For example, our mission at Focus on the Family is evangelism, and our means is to address a host of family issues. The family is an institution created by God, and His principles allow it to function well. Those who do not follow Christ will have a difficult time following His principles for family living, so our radio programs and publications regularly appeal to people to adopt not only Christ's principles but also Christ Himself.

This is our call—the life of the family. There are many issues that deal only indirectly with the health of the family, so we generally stay out of them. I'm referring to matters with important moral implications, such as the environment, civil rights, poverty, national defense, capital punishment, economic policies (except for the tax burden on families), immigration, and genetic research. We realize that for each of these issues one can make a convincing argument about how families are affected. But they are not as central to family health as the matters on which we concentrate. Furthermore, for each of the issues cited, there are many organizations, often secular ones, that are already tackling the problems. So there is simply less need for our help, given our limited resources.

SORTING IT OUT

At the end of this book, in Appendix B, there is a plan for how you can get your church involved in issues of righteousness. And here are some questions for determining how you personally might become involved appropriately and effectively in moral issues.

First, do you have useful experience in an issue? Often the most effective participants in a godly cause have known the problem intimately. Some of the strongest opponents of pornography in their communities are people who themselves have had an addiction to pornography and understand firsthand its corrosive nature. Phil Burress is a Cincinnati activist with a pornography addiction in his past. Not only has he conquered it with God's intervention in his life but he has also become adept at keeping pornography out of many communities in his area. His story is told in Appendix A-3.

Likewise, many fervent pro-life activists are those who themselves have had abortions and suffered the subsequent emotional pain of having willfully killed their unborn children. These women know that the rhetoric of the pro-abortion movement is fraudulent and that the procedure is neither painless nor without long-lasting emotional consequences. Thousands of local crisis pregnancy centers are staffed by employees and volunteers who have known the issue firsthand.

Unfortunate experiences such as abortions and addictions show the truth of the scriptural passage that says "in all things God works for the good of those who love him" (Romans 8:28).

Second, has God planted in you a heart for lost people? Remember that the first and most important matter to be made right—that is to say, it needs to meet God's standard of righteousness—is an individual's relationship with Him. This is the need for salvation. People who have a passion for the lost frequently shy away from activities that bring them into contact with opponents, fearing that a confrontation might harm an opportunity for the gospel. Often, however, an issue that is controversial in the news looks much different in person.

Abortion is such an issue. In the great debates about abortion, particularly in the heat of election campaigns, the rhetoric can grow harsh. But at the local level, where most people plug in, it is commonly not so. Sydna Masse, a pro-life consultant and teacher, says many pregnant women come into a crisis pregnancy center for a free pregnancy test and discover a world they never knew existed. Many are grateful for the help they find, and some are led to Christ.

The controversy over homosexuality is another issue in which the stridency of the national debate masks the evangelistic ministry that often takes place one on one. Typical of many gay men, Donnie struggled for years with his sexual failure, but finally he found a ministry to gays in Denver called Where Grace Abounds. He began to improve after he made a crucial decision. "In my mind I said ... my goal is not to be straight; it's to figure out who God is.... Once I did that, I felt myself changing and growing."[2]

Gay activists heap scorn on people like Donnie, and on ministries like the one in Denver, because anyone who leaves homosexuality provides evidence that it is not an innate, unchangeable characteristic like racial identity. Hence the activist campaign for special civil rights protection is undermined. Many times the route out of homosexuality passes through Christian ministries, and conversion to Christ is an essential step. People committed to personal evangelism can find many opportunities in spite of the controversies surrounding divisive issues.

Third, what role suits your personality? Regardless of the issue you're drawn toward, what part should you play in it? Some roles require a measure of tact and diplomacy because they involve contact with the press, government officials, and the public. Those who speak "Christianese" will be of little help in dealing with the secular news media. Many Christians travel exclusively in church circles and don't realize how strange it sounds to an outsider when we use such phrases as "the Lord spoke to me," "washed in the blood," or "accepting Jesus." The media simply won't understand or won't accept as credible what is being said. By the same measure, someone whose first impulse is to try to convert a reporter to Christianity rather than explain a position on an issue probably won't be effective in either task.

On the other hand, sometimes a personality unsuitable for the front line can be the key to success. Some years ago, Deb and I were part of a group of parents who wanted to show our local school board that we were unhappy with the sex education program at the middle school. Part of our strategy was to get parents in the community to sign a petition, and one of our group was a plainspoken mother with a blunt and confrontational style. She stood for several hours at the entrance to a local supermarket, not a bit shy about flagging down stranger after stranger, and she collected more signatures than we could have imagined.

Fourth, how much time do you have? Life circumstances often determine what one can do. A mother at home with young children will have less time than later in life when the children are grown. In fact, more and more people are beginning second careers in Christian work of all sorts after their children are out of the house. You should never discount the value of a phone call, letter, or e-mail to a political or business leader on a topic of concern. The reason that small efforts are so significant is that few people do even this much.

Fifth, what skills do you have? If an organized campaign is required to change a government policy or to prevent a bad piece of legislation from becoming enacted, many skills must be brought to the table. There must be an overall strategy, a plan for raising money, an effective public relations scheme, and a credible organization for managing all of this. (Read about a young Christian mother who brought her writing skill to the fight against slavery and wrote what became one of the most powerful books in American history. Her story is told in Appendix A-2.) Unfortunately, many people who take on moral issues don't think about these things ahead of time. They jump into action with great enthusiasm and high emotions. Frequently the task demands more than they have to give, and the result is burnout or demoralization.

On the other hand, when preparation is thorough, the results can be remarkable. In 1991, a measure appeared on the election ballot in Washington state that would have legalized doctor-assisted suicide. Its advocates chose Washington because the state leans politically leftward, and preelection polls showed that euthanasia might win by as much as 30 percent. Pro-life and pro-family organizations knew they had a fight on their hands. They organized well, worked through many differences of opinion about strategy, and paid for sophisticated polling and a professional advertising consultant. They located an unassailable spokesman to be the campaign's public voice—a hospice nurse with 10 years' experience caring for terminally ill patients. Since this was a medical matter, a physician organized a group of doctors to speak against the measure and to meet with newspaper editorial boards.

In addition, these wise opponents realized from their polling data that they couldn't win if they tried to convince voters that euthanasia was morally wrong. The best they could hope for was to plant doubts about the particular measure on the ballot, and they did indeed find a hole in it. It was written broadly enough so that technically even a patient's eye doctor could legally kill him. The opponents also drew attention to how proper pain management could eliminate a patient's desire to end his life, and they questioned whether a physician who fumbled this protocol could be entrusted with doctor-assisted suicide.

Finally, the opponents stormed heaven. Pastors from each of Washington's 39 counties gathered at the state capitol to lead 40 days of nonstop, round-the-clock prayer vigils by a host of volunteers from about 100 denominations and Christian organizations. On election day, 68 percent of the state's voters turned out, a 20-year high for a nonpresidential election year. The suicide ballot measure was defeated by a solid eight percentage points—a result that could not have been imagined when the campaign against the measure began.

The campaign against legalized suicide in Washington illustrates the importance of skill and experience in the pursuit of a righteous cause, but over the years I have seen such skill all too infrequently. More often I have witnessed poorly prepared people taking on issues of immense size, hoping that somehow God will do a miracle. Sometimes they emphasize prayer meetings more than street-level organization, and that just does not work, I'm sorry to say.

I wish that God would answer prayers for miraculous intervention in an ill-planned campaign, but in my experience He doesn't, and who could really have expected anything different? Suppose, for example, that prayer vigils were organized for someone's delicate surgery, but the surgery was performed by a writer instead of a surgeon. It would be the height of spiritual arrogance to expect God to answer prayers in that circumstance. Yet many people do exactly that when they take on complicated public policy issues in which proper preparation is neglected.

Many people who are neither grassroots troops nor leaders on whom the spotlight is trained are nonetheless vital to every organization. These are people who occupy boards of directors—folks with the business, financial, and organizational skills to ensure that the campaign is run properly, the supply lines filled and the bills paid, so the doors can remain open and the campaign can succeed. Boards meet only on occasion, but they are vital. People who have boardroom skills ought to take seriously the unique roles they are able to play. Here are some qualities of good board members:

1. Wisdom, usually the product of long years in leading a successful enterprise.

2. An even-tempered personality.
3. The desire to work for the good of the organization rather than seek personal advancement.
4. Spiritual maturity.
5. The patience and vision to concentrate on the big picture and the long term rather than the more exciting and immediate projects and problems of the day.
6. Business, finance, or fund-raising skills.

Finally, to what are you committed? What is your calling from God? What has moved you? What has assaulted your sense of justice, compassion, or fairness, even though you may have absolutely no experience or skill on a particular subject? Often it is sheer determination that conquers a host of inadequacies.

In the early 1990s, we began hearing from parents around the country and in Canada about a new language arts program called *Impressions* from a leading textbook publisher, Harcourt Brace Jovanovich. Its goal was good, to get more children reading, but some of the stories were badly scaring the children. There were tales of ghouls, pigs with a taste for children's flesh, spell casting and the occult, and cannibalism. Most of the parents we talked to had no idea how to confront the issue of curriculum selection, and when they tried to speak up, they were branded by school authorities as censors.

A parents' group in Calgary, Alberta, began digging into the question of just what were the educational standards for curricula in their schools, and they learned a lot. They had the school district ask the publisher why *Impressions* contained such morbid selections, and Harcourt said simply that children seemed to like frightening stories. One of the Calgary parents confronted the school board about it. As he recalled later: "I said, 'Are you actually telling me that you allow the children to establish their own curriculum? Children like chocolate too, but you don't let them eat it for breakfast, lunch, and dinner.' They didn't answer me. They just looked a little sheepish. What could they say?"[3]

Gradually, guided by several in-depth articles in *Citizen* magazine, the parental uprising in various cities began to take hold, and the publisher went on the defensive, even publishing a guide for how school authorities should respond to parental complaints. But the determination of parents to protect their children eventually overwhelmed the publisher and the academic "experts" in the school districts, and the series was withdrawn.

Here's another example of God-given compassion. The pro-life issue is one that moves many people, and in 1991 and 1992 a group of Christians in California made a remarkable impact on this issue without noise, picketing, or protesting. All they did was pray and talk quietly to women at 100 abortion clinics around the state. Many mothers who were intending to enter those clinics during the prayer vigils were moved to rethink their decisions. After speaking to sidewalk counselors about the realities of abortion, they went instead to pro-life crisis pregnancy centers for help. Many babies were saved, and the pro-life centers were inundated. They provided help with pro-life doctors, along with information about housing, clothing, furniture, financing, and churches. The prayer vigils were so effective that one abortion clinic shut its doors during the event. Another clinic director promised to refer to the pro-lifers any mother who seemed in doubt about her abortion decision, and several medical centers decided to stop performing abortions permanently. All this was accomplished by people with a burden for the unborn and a burden for prayer.

Sometimes people take up a cause for which they have absolutely no background; they are equipped only with determination. Dr. Richard Neill is a dentist in Fort Worth who, in 1992, was bothered by the fact that the raunchy *Donahue* program aired in Fort Worth at nine A.M. and was watched by an estimated 10,000 children a day. Although he was irritated, like most people he didn't do anything about it. Then one evening he heard a speech on community activism, so he began circulating petitions in churches to convince the Dallas/Fort Worth station at least to move the program to a late-night time slot. Although he turned in 9,000 signatures, the station refused to act, citing the show's popularity.

Next, Neill began watching the program so he could jot down the names of advertisers. He called corporate offices to get the names and titles of executives. Then he began writing polite letters, accurately describing offensive scenes on the program, and he requested that the advertisers withdraw. He recorded a 22-minute video of shocking scenes and sent that along as well. He set a goal of convincing four advertisers to sign off by year's end, but an astonishing 91 local and national advertisers pulled out as a result of his work. Among them were some of the country's largest consumer advertisers. One of them, Sara Lee, said through a spokesman that Neill's letters were always well written, that he stuck to the facts, and that he accurately named the products. Because he did his work well, the company paid attention, and the spokesman credited Neill with helping it to do the right thing by dropping the program.

Dr. Neill kept on writing, and advertisers kept on canceling their commercials. By spring 1993, 143 companies had written him to say they no longer would advertise on the program, including *Donahue*'s top sponsor, Kraft General Foods, which had spent $2.7 million on the program in just six months during 1992. The program host, Phil Donahue, called Neill a "pip-squeak" in a *TV Guide* interview, but his distribution company acknowledged that the hemorrhage of advertising dollars had grown critical.

Donahue had no choice but to take on the dentist directly by broadcasting a program from Fort Worth. He invited Neill to fill half of the audience at the county convention center and join the program as a guest. Neill declined, certain he wouldn't get a fair hearing after noting that the program's title was to be "Crusading Christians Who Hate Phil." Donahue's stunt proved futile, and eventually the program left the air. Donahue, of course, attributed the cancellation to reasons other than the persistent dentist from Fort Worth who just wouldn't give up.

YOUR TURN

These, then, are examples of everyday people who took on causes much larger than themselves. As this book comes to a close, my advice to you is simple: Go and do likewise. If you do, you will never regret it. Take your stand for righteousness in an arena suited to you. Find others who will join with you (see Appendix B). Pray for God's leading and listen closely to His call. If you follow that call, your Christian life will grow richer and deeper than you ever imagined, because you will see firsthand how critically important are Christ's principles of righteousness in this fallen world.

Society desperately seeks the answers you have. The world needs your salt. The world needs your light. But make no mistake. If you do step into an arena in which God's truth is facing the agents of spiritual darkness, you may be pummeled, and you may be bruised, if not physically then emotionally. So were most of the people described in this chapter, who were unknown and untried when they drew their line in the dust and said, "The evil goes no further. I will fight it." They persisted and ultimately won their day for the Lord.

If you do this work, you will be standing on the broad shoulders of many who have gone before you, who contended with the same foreboding and misgiving that you will experience. As this book has shown, down through history God's people have carried His banner into one dangerous arena after another. They stood for righteousness, not because any of them were well trained or well funded, but because they found it to be the right thing to do. They learned as they went, and the most important lesson they learned was to lean on God. As they did, they found His blessings and mercies in abundance, fully sufficient for the tasks they faced.

And now it is your turn. I do not believe that you read this far by accident. I believe you're holding this book now because God has appointed you and has an assignment for you in an arena of righteousness. Do not miss this divine opportunity to experience God working through you, to be His instrument at this critical moment in history.

APPENDICES

American Case Studies

APPENDIX A-1
Theodore Weld's Crusade Against Slavery

COTTON WAS BECOMING THE KING OF AMERICAN exports early in the nineteenth century when a spiritual revival began to break loose across the young nation, a great inundation of the Spirit known as the Second Great Awakening. That flood was to engulf a 29-year-old lawyer living in upstate New York, a man named Charles Finney, who, on a crisp October day in 1821, found himself in a woods near his law office trying to get right with God. Finney had read his Bible and had listened carefully in church, but what he had heard from the pulpit was the thin, whistling wind of stunted Calvinism that for a long time now had been blowing out of spiritually cold New England. This brand of intellectualized Christianity was lifeless, and Finney thought there must be more to Christianity. When he read his Bible, Finney found the message from a God who yearned for a warm, living, and growing relationship. On his knees in the woods that day, Finney was so broken by the weight of his sins that he cried aloud.

Finney converted to genuine faith, and he never looked back. He would no longer practice law but became instead the greatest revivalist of his era. His message was that the salvation of the soul represents not the finished work of a predestined state but rather the beginning of a sanctified life, a life evidenced by holy works that please God. All sin, he said, is selfishness. Holiness, by contrast, consists of living a life of "disinterested benevolence." Calvinism had made salvation the end of all human desire, and fear of hell the spur to belief, whereas Finney regarded salvation as only the beginning of religious experience. Converts, he declared, did not escape life; they began a new life ... "useful in the highest degree possible."[1]

Finney's concepts left an indelible mark on the country's understanding of Christianity, and his fiery revival preaching ignited a fuse that exploded into an era of social reform. His preaching would bring the Second Great Awakening to fullness, shaping American Christianity as a divine engine for removing the greatest social evil the nation had ever known.

Finney's revivals set New York ablaze, and over the course of his career a half million people were converted—many of them long-standing churchgoers who had never consciously accepted the message of Christ. Finney invited talented and enthusiastic new converts to join his "holy band" of helpers, to the dismay of stodgy clergymen whose churches often seemed to have been invaded by a band of spiritual lunatics— "enthusiasts," as they were politely called—after Finney whirled into town.

THE LEADER OF THE HOLY BAND

One of the most enthusiastic of Finney's holy band was an extraordinary young man named Theodore Weld. Weld had been born in Connecticut in 1803, the son and grandson of Congregational ministers. As the offspring of stern Puritan stock, he grew up in the same world of rigid rules and stiff theology that Finney had known. Weld showed himself to be enterprising and intelligent, taking charge of a 100-acre farm in order to earn his way into Phillips Academy at the age of 16. His unusual gift for public speaking made itself known early, and when eyesight problems hampered his college studies, he prepared a series of lectures on the science of mnemonics—the improvement of memory—and took to the road.

He traveled across New York, Pennsylvania, Washington, D.C., and into the American South. He found that he could indeed hold the attention of his audiences, even though he was only 17. It was on his speaking tour in the Southern states that Weld got his first glimpse of slavery, and he was disturbed deeply by what he saw: one man buying and selling another, chaining him like an animal, and torturing and killing him at whim.

A CHRISTIAN TAKES A STAND

After his conversion, Weld leaped into a new life of Christian service. Like many in Finney's holy band, he needed the tempering of formal theological study. He enrolled in a Bible school, but his prodigious talents could not be contained. During vacations he rejoined Finney's band of preachers, and he also found time to take up the cause of temperance. His gifts of persuasion were so remarkable that after his sermons, liquor dealers were said to return home and empty their whiskey barrels into the streets.

The young preacher's reputation grew, and he was sought out by well-known ministers to lead revivals in their towns. But they weren't the only ones who saw promise in Theodore Weld. So did a wealthy Christian benefactor named Lewis Tappan, a New York City merchant and founder of a company that would become known as Dun & Bradstreet. Tappan implored Weld, who was not yet 30 years old, to come to New York and convert the entire city. "Do what may be done elsewhere, and leave this city the headquarters of Satan, and the nation is not saved," Tappan wrote Weld. But Weld insisted that the great West (then Ohio, Indiana, and Illinois) was more important for the future of the gospel and the country. He told Tappan the region needed a seminary.[2]

Weld got his way when Tappan arranged the financing for Lane Seminary in Cincinnati and, with an eye for quality, searched out the best man he could find to serve as its president. He settled on the Boston pulpiteer and moral reformer Lyman Beecher. Weld was offered a place on the Lane faculty, as professor of sacred rhetoric and oratory, but in characteristic self-effacement he declined. Instead, he enrolled as an ordinary student, along with dozens of other Finney converts. The Lane Seminary freshman class of 1833 was 93 men strong, the largest and most impressive body of theological students that had ever gathered in America.

By drawing these students to Cincinnati, Lane Seminary guaranteed trouble for itself. The city lay on the northern bank of the Ohio River, and on the opposite bank lay the slave state of Kentucky. Although Ohio was free, Cincinnati commerce depended on the goods and services of the slave-owning South, and slave traders dragged chained escapees through Cincinnati back to the South. The city was also home for more than a third of the 7,500 free blacks in Ohio,[3] most of whom had struggled out of slavery, one way or another. All in all, Cincinnati was a living laboratory for the study of slavery and what it did to people.

The Lane students, zealous with the love of Christ, quickly established relationships with these black residents. For his part, Weld lived, ate, and worshiped in the black community. Weld lost his heart to these people, who were destitute but industrious. He wrote a letter about what he learned:

> I visited this week about 30 families and found that some
> members of more than half these families were still in
> bondage.... I found one man paying for his wife and five chil-
> dren; they had just redeemed the last, and had paid for them-
> selves and children $1,400. Another woman recently paid the
> last installment of the purchase money for her husband. She
> had purchased him by taking in washing, and working late at
> night, after performing as help at hard work. But I cannot tell
> half.... After spending three or four hours and getting facts, I
> was forced to stop from sheer heartache and agony.[4]

The Slavery Debate

The Lane students asked for permission to debate the slavery issue on campus, but Lyman Beecher, Lane's president, demurred. Only a few years before, race riots had broken out in Cincinnati as a result of the white population's increasing nervousness about so many freed slaves living there.

The most troubling part was that some of the town's respected citizens, not just riverfront ruffians, were observed in the mob. Beecher was torn between his reformer's heart and his desire to maintain peace. But since Arthur Tappan, the seminary's benefactor, was an ardent abolitionist, Beecher nervously told the students to proceed.

For 18 nights, the students gathered to address all aspects of the question. As the debate started, most of them, like Northerners generally, opposed abolition. They thought it sheer madness to suddenly set 2 million illiterate and untrained slaves loose upon the land. Their preferred solution was colonization—an almost totally unworkable scheme by which slaves would be banished to the African colony of Liberia.[5]

The dominant intellect in the debate was Weld's. He influenced his fellow students not only by his detailed knowledge of slavery but also by his kindness and his willingness to hear all viewpoints. When the dust had settled, he had won the allegiance of the entire student body. One of the students, reflecting back on the debate, wrote of Weld: "He ... uttered no malice; sharpened no phrase so that its venomed point might rankle in another's breast.... His great soul was full of compassion for the oppressor and the oppressed.... Nobly simple in manner, free from thought of self, he touched the springs of the human heart."[6]

THE GREAT CHRISTIAN CAMPAIGN

The first hint of the troubles that loomed ahead occurred shortly after the Lane students reached their verdict in favor of abolition. The seminary trustees, cowering in the face of the anger rising in Cincinnati from this student "agitation," demanded that all the discussion cease, that the abolition society begun by the students be disbanded, and that the students end their efforts to lift the city's blacks from the oppression of poverty. Do all of this, said the trustees, or face dismissal. In unison, the students resigned and walked out of the seminary. Some of them stayed in Cincinnati to minister to the city's poor, but the bulk of them enrolled in Oberlin College, a new academic enterprise in northern Ohio. Following these events closely from New York, Arthur Tappan not only made a generous cash gift to Oberlin but also persuaded none other than Charles Finney to join the college as a professor. Later he would become its president.

Lyman Beecher, now the president of a school without students, was bereft, having been unable to make peace between the forces of abolition on his campus and those in the larger circles of northern society who salved their consciences with the concept of colonization. Even Beecher's children, all but one having participated nightly in the controversy at the Beecher dinner table, went over to the abolitionist cause. One of them, Harriet, who was married to a Lane professor named Calvin Stowe, drank deeply of these years in Cincinnati and in the future would gather her insights into a novel. (See Appendix A-2.)

During the Lane debate, Weld had exhibited great command of the facts about the horrors of slavery. But the centerpiece of his message was simply that slavery was a sin, and he denounced it "always, everywhere, and only" a sin. One historian states: "The anti-slavery movement was a powerful religious crusade.... The Bible was presented as irrefutable proof that Jesus taught a doctrine of universal brotherhood; that man was created in the image of God, and that slavery reduced him to a piece of merchandise to be bought and sold in the marketplace."[7]

Actually, the Bible teaches only the brotherhood of those who believe in Christ. But that error notwithstanding, historians are clear that Bible-believing Christians such as Weld provided the dominant force that called the country to account about the great evil of slavery. When the American Anti-Slavery Society was organized in 1833, its executive committee said, "Every man who has put on the armor of Jesus Christ is under the paramount pledge to do all in his power for the salvation of the souls for which He died. How can you, my brother, do more than by now espousing the cause of those for whose souls there are no men to care?"

SPREADING THE GOSPEL OF ABOLITION

After leaving Lane Seminary in 1834, Weld became an agent of the American Anti-Slavery Society. His first target was Ohio, but as he would soon learn, not even this northern state would be easily corralled to the cause of immediate emancipation.

Certainly the nation, in the tender years of the 1830s, was more consistently Christian than it is today. Still, the task of spreading the abolitionist message across the North was extremely difficult, and the abolitionists were able to make steady though painful progress only because Weld and other leaders were willing to commit themselves to the cause in spite of tremendous cost to themselves. They also made progress because Weld set a marvelous example of godliness in the face of mounting violence against the abolitionists.

Weld toured town after town, an evangelist for abolition, speaking each night for two to five hours, never exhausting his subject, and molding his work after Finney's revival meetings. Opposition was fierce. Arriving in a new town, he usually found that he could get through the first night's message in a church without incident. But invariably, when word of his sermon spread around town, a mob formed and barred him from using any local church again. So he spoke on succeeding nights in a barn or warehouse, or in the open, wherever he could gather his audience. Once he was able to get a hearing, he won many converts, and local anti-slavery societies sprang to life wherever he preached.

Physical danger was constant. Repeatedly, he was stoned. "At Circleville, a large rock crashed through the church window: 'one so well aimed,' wrote Weld, 'that it struck me on the head and for a moment stunned me. [I] paused for a moment until the dizziness had ceased, then went on and finished my lecture. Meanwhile some of the gentlemen had hung their cloaks up at the window so that my head could not so easily be used as a target. The injury was not serious, though for a few days I had frequent turns of dizziness.' "[8]

The most dangerous times came when he emerged from his early meetings in any location before winning enough converts to form a bodyguard against the mob. When surrounded, he simply folded his arms and waded straight through, suffering what blows he must. After one night's harrowing walk, he wrote, "The Lord restrained them, not a hair of my head was injured."[9]

At Painesville, Ohio, bedlam broke loose when a mob invaded the church where Weld was preaching. Among the assailants were two men bearing a large bass drum, which they beat repeatedly. Weld spoke louder. One of the drum bearers gradually became interested in what Weld was saying, and he asked his partner to stop beating the drum. They got into an argument, and finally the first man kicked in the drumhead so he could hear Weld better.

In the spring of 1835, Weld journeyed to Zanesville to organize a state antislavery society, but no one would allow him to lecture anywhere in town. He retreated across the Muskingum River to tiny Putnam, where he was given access to a public room, and his usual welcome ensued. After his first lecture, the hall was stormed by a mob that shattered windows, beat down the door, and engulfed him with stones and clubs as he emerged. Remarkably, he again escaped unharmed, and before he left town, he achieved his purpose. The Ohio Anti-Slavery Society was formed.

THE DIFFICULT CAMPAIGN

Quickly it became apparent to Weld that he would need more help, and he knew immediately where to find it. He visited Oberlin, which was fast becoming a center for Christian reform causes, and he performed one of the more remarkable feats in the history of American preaching. For 21 straight nights, Weld lectured on abolition in Oberlin's cold, dingy chapel. Even for the gifted Weld, it was a superb performance. He wrote Tappan that "you may judge something of the interest when I tell you that from five to six hundred males and females attended every night, and sit shivering ... without anything to lean back against."[10]

Characteristically, he wasn't telling the half of it. One member of the audience was James Fairchild, a sophomore student at the time and eventually a professor and then president of Oberlin. Weld's biographer wrote that Weld's "excoriation of slavery was an experience [Fairchild] never forgot. Fairchild doubted if any community was ever more profoundly moved by the eloquence of a single man. College students and [townspeople] alike sat spellbound. Studies suffered, but Fairchild thought Weld's lectures were an education in themselves. Weld gave Oberlin such an antislavery baptism that it was ever after an abolition citadel."[11] When

Weld finished his series of lectures, he had six solid recruits, all of them rebels from Lane Seminary in Cincinnati, and all of them eager to join the fray.

Through Ohio they went, getting stoned, clubbed, and cursed, but also winning converts by the hundreds because the speakers would neither be intimidated nor leave town. They simply took their punishment as a cost of doing the Lord's business, and eventually they outlasted the anger of the mobs. It was, however, a wearisome business. The abolitionists were pelted with rotten eggs so often that one of them, James Thone, began claiming that rotten eggs hatched abolitionists, so numerous were both the eggs and the converts.

On and on they went, through Ohio and into Pennsylvania, where Weld and his associates won great numbers of converts without being assailed by mobs. The torments returned, however, when Weld entered New York, preaching in the same upstate cities where Finney had ignited the great Christian revival only a decade before. To his surprise, Weld won over Utica, where hundreds were turned away during his 16 nights of meetings. Only four months before, a mob in that city had driven out the state antislavery convention. Rochester and Buffalo converted easily, but then the resistance stiffened and the mobs began forming again. "At Lockport county officials led the rioters, and they ceased their disorders only when they found they must kill Weld in order to silence him."[12]

At Troy, a furious storm broke upon him. Historian Gilbert Barnes tells the tale:

> Here was stationed Dr. Beman, in whose church Finney had preached during the Great Revival. Like all of Finney's colleagues he was an abolitionist; but his tone was pugnacious and irascible, and his agitation had only increased hostility throughout the city. When Weld came he found the entire city already provoked against his cause, ready for any extreme of violence.... The mayor expressed regret that he did not have the power to remove Weld bodily from the city, ... and the public crier with his bell summoned a mob.... At Weld's first meeting, rioters led by a city official invaded the church and surged up the aisles

toward the speaker. Three times they attacked the pulpit and were thrice repulsed by his fighting bodyguard of young men, with casualties on both sides. The frightened mayor, repenting his heated words, called the city council to his aid and after meeting the city fathers escorted Weld to his lodging amid a shower of stones.

Weld chose to remain in the city and face the mob until violence was exhausted and he could get a hearing; but it was a perilous business. When he appeared on the streets, surrounded though he was by a bodyguard, mobs gathered to stone him, and he was struck repeatedly. After a few days of this, his entire body was "one general, painful bruise," and several times he narrowly escaped more serious injury. Despite the pleas of his friends and the protests of the authorities, he determined to remain until either his life or mob violence had ended. He canceled engagements elsewhere and ... wrote a farewell letter. In it, he said, "Let every abolitionist debate the matter once and for all, and settle it with himself ... whether he can stand to lie upon the rack ... and tread with steady step the scaffold— whether he can stand at the post of duty and having done all and suffered all ... fall and die a martyr.... God gird us all to do valiantly for the helpless and innocent. Blessed are they who die in the harness." Violence did not die nor did Weld. The city fathers finally offered him the alternative of voluntary or forcible removal, and, resigned to reality, he departed, having failed for the first time to conciliate hostility and win a hearing for immediatism.[13]

Although he failed in Troy, Weld's zeal for New York won thousands to the cause of abolition across the state. It was a tremendous triumph, but it came at great cost to Weld. He was debilitated, worn down by the physical assaults during his relentless speaking schedule. His voice was reduced to a gravelly croak, the result of so many nights of shouting above mobs.

But he won so many converts that the American Anti-Slavery Society decided in 1836 to expand the number of itinerant abolitionist agents to 70, the size of Christ's company of disciples. Weld was asked to gather the new recruits and train them. Physically spent, Weld gamely responded to this new challenge by gathering the Lane rebels once again. He recruited other seminary students as well, and even ordained ministers, for an intensive two-week training session. "Gaunt and battered, his voice ragged ... he never spoke with greater power. Day and night for two weeks, scarcely allowing time to eat, he filled the seventy with facts and fervor."[14]

THE HUMBLE LEADER

That was to be the end of Weld's public speaking career; his voice never fully recovered. Yet rarely had a man spent himself in a greater cause or with so much to show for it. In his short crusade across Ohio, Pennsylvania, and New York, this remarkable and almost totally unrecognized apostle of human freedom planted seeds that were soon to take firm root, sprout, and bear fruit abundantly in the growing national struggle against slavery. And above all else, Weld exemplified the character of Christ.

He possessed astounding humility. It cost him a larger place in the annals of the abolitionists, but he would not have cared. Everything he wrote he researched painstakingly, yet he frequently used pseudonyms to avoid drawing attention to himself. Instead of becoming a professor at Lane Seminary, he enrolled as a student. When he was asked to address the American Anti-Slavery Society's annual meeting in New York, he declined. When he was asked to speak to the Rhode Island Legislature, he said no. When similar requests came from Pennsylvania and Connecticut, he turned them down. He was invited to London to address the British Antislavery Society, and he refused. He declined every opportunity to run any abolitionist organization.

To all of these honors and opportunities for advancement, Weld's response was always the same: He believed himself called to preach in the backcountry and small towns, and that is what he did. The resolve that kept him from stepping to center stage was forged from the same iron that held him steadfast at the pulpit when the rocks and eggs flew. He simply would not be deterred, not by high honor, by high danger, or by the loss of his speaking voice.

WELD'S NEW VOICE

The 70 abolitionist agents trained by Weld fanned out across the North and built upon his work, reaping even more converts to the cause and laying the groundwork for a broad new phase of the abolition campaign. Still, neither major party in Congress would deal with the slavery issue. Since the Lane Seminary uprising, Theodore Weld and his abolitionist disciples had inflamed the West with their passion and logic. They had planted hundreds of antislavery societies, which sent millions of petitions to Washington, pressing for an end to slavery. But Congress was controlled by Democrats who abhorred abolitionists, and by Whigs who mostly tried not to notice, even though the cascade of petitions implored them to do so. House leaders devised a "gag rule" by which they tabled debate on antislavery petitions.

By squelching the petitions, the House leaders brought one of the old lions of politics roaring back to life. John Quincy Adams, who had served as the sixth president and then had been elected to the House, was not himself an abolitionist but was deeply offended that the people's elected representatives rebuffed their petitions. He lived up to his nickname "Old Man Eloquent" as he railed and raged and connived, with his great grasp of parliamentary procedure, to introduce the petitions and debate them at every turn.

Adams didn't lack ammunition for his fusillades. Neither did Congressman Joshua Giddings, one of several influential Weld disciples in Washington. For they summoned the man who knew most about the issue of slavery—Theodore Weld himself.

Weld arrived from New York, where he had become a walking encyclopedia on the subject of slavery and had written, among many articles and publications, the most devastatingly detailed attack on slavery ever published, *Slavery As It Is*. Immensely influential, it sold more than 100,000 copies in the first year alone and was popular in Britain as well. Charles Dickens borrowed entirely from it for a chapter in his *American Notes*, without acknowledging the source. Weld evidently didn't care. Characteristically, he didn't allow his own name to be put on the book.

To prepare the book, Weld, his wife, and her sister had culled through proslavery Southern newspapers for details on slavery as the papers were discarded from a New York City library. In six months' time they had paged through 20,000 papers, producing an indictment against slavery that had come from the slaveholders themselves. He commuted weekly into the city from his farm upstate, and when in New York, he took meals with a black couple in a run-down, drafty little room. He slept two miles away in a tiny attic. He was up at dawn for an hour of exercise before breakfast and was at his desk by eight each day. After work he visited ill and impoverished black residents nearby, and he never retired before 11 P.M.[15]

Armed with all his knowledge and his prodigious work habits, Weld was an ample source of facts and strategy for the heated congressional debates against slavery. The abolitionists in Congress attacked on many fronts. They argued that Congress must eradicate slavery from the District of Columbia, the city administered by Congress. They pressed for no new slave states to be admitted to the Union. They argued that slaves who escaped from ships having run aground outside U.S. jurisdiction were free, and owners had no right to ask for federal authorities to recover them. What the abolitionists never claimed was that slavery was illegal in slave states, because there was general consensus that the federal government had no authority to dictate policy to existing states, even on a matter as urgent as this.

A NEW PARTY EMERGES

But in 1854, Sen. Stephen A. Douglas, a Democrat, proposed that "popular sovereignty" over slavery be instituted as the territories of Kansas and Nebraska became states. Antislavery people were horrified, because this meant that if the local citizens wanted slavery, two new slave states would be carved out of the Western territories in violation of national policy.[16]

In a dramatic response, antislavery leaders in Congress issued an appeal to the people, laying out the double cross and the threat to peace if the law should pass. It was written by Giddings and edited by Senators Samuel Chase of Ohio and Charles Sumner of Massachusetts. Reprinted widely in northern newspapers, it closed with an appeal to conscience:

> We implore Christians and Christian ministers to interpose. Their divine religion requires them to behold in every man a brother, and to labor for the advancement and regeneration of the human race.... For ourselves, we shall resist it by speech and vote, and with all the abilities which God has given us. Even if overcome in the impending struggle, we shall not submit. We shall go home to our constituents, erect anew the standard of freedom, and call on the people to come to the rescue of the country from the domination of slavery. We will not despair; for the cause of human freedom is the cause of God.[17]

The appeal inflamed the North anew against slavery, but the measure passed nonetheless in the Democrat-dominated Congress. In the ensuing political melee over the Kansas-Nebraska controversy, the Whig Party dissolved and the northern Democrats who opposed slavery at last surrendered all pretense of being able to rescue their party from the iron grip of the Southern planters. President Franklin Pierce (a Democrat) signed the bill into law, and a broad new political alliance started to congeal around opposition to this "slave power." In late 1854 it took on the name of the Republican Party, and it prepared for ultimate confrontation with the South.

The abolitionists who had at first inflamed the struggle for freedom out of biblical convictions saw their pure sentiments engulfed by broader considerations. As they drew in more and more people, the antislavery agenda took on new and sometimes sour notes. There was fear of the growing power of the planter class. There was concern that the economic engine of slave labor would undermine the opportunity for family farms and would keep small businesses from flourishing. There was also the ugliness of white supremacy, festering from the notion that the fertile new states were destined to be owned by white farmers and ranchers, not worked by black slaves under the thumb of rich Southern aristocrats.

Hostilities grew. With the passage of the Kansas-Nebraska Act, free-staters and proslavery settlers hotfooted it to the new territories. Kansas politics degenerated into guerrilla warfare.

Most abolitionists were shocked. None of these developments could have been foreseen 20 years ago when they began preaching the pure gospel of God's love for all human beings. Were these political developments good or were they evil? Was it better to tolerate wrong means while working toward a noble end, or was it better to stay pure and on the sidelines? Was all of this hate and bloodshed merely God's inevitable revenge for the human misery inflicted by white men upon black men?

Weld left Washington in 1843. The politicians, including Giddings, stayed in the fight. In the summer of 1856, the new Republican Party nominated the celebrated western adventurer and pathfinder John C. Frémont. He lost the election. But in four more years, with no hope that the North and the South could find civilized means to bridge the widening gulf, the Republican Party prevailed, and President Abraham Lincoln was shortly presiding over a nation at war with itself.

SIX LESSONS LEARNED

The long, difficult campaign to free the slaves is an unparalleled object lesson for those of us who are gravely concerned about evil in our country today and who wonder about the role Christianity should play in addressing those problems. Here are six lessons to be learned from the abolition movement:

1. Revival brought trouble, not bliss. Today many Christians yearn for God to bring a revival in the land. They believe that when many hearts turn toward the Lord, things will be much better in our society. They say that evangelism is the paramount work of the church and that forays into divisive social issues only turn people away from the gospel.

These people have it backward. In the abolition campaign, controversy didn't squelch evangelism; evangelism opened people's eyes to evil, and that *started* the controversy. It all began with Finney's preaching at the peak of a revival, the Second Great Awakening. In great numbers, people were won to Christ. But newly motivated Christians began to look at the evil world through fresh eyes, and they plunged in where evil abounded.

Abolition addressed the greatest evil of the day, but there were many reform movements spawned by the movement of the Spirit at that time. As people confronted evil, controversies didn't cease; they rose, because righteousness always divides people. Many fought the reforms out of prejudice, ignorance, greed, or philosophical differences. Theodore Weld found it physically dangerous to try to get a hearing against slavery even in northern churches. These Christians had seared their consciences against the reality of slavery by passing the plate once a year in a foolish campaign to buy freedom for slaves and deport them to Africa. As Weld awakened people to the sin of slavery, he jarred their complacency, and that is always controversial.

2. A common goal brought conflicting motives. As the abolition movement spread, it thinned, and this troubled the purists in the movement. They championed immediate freedom for black people for only one reason: Human dignity was a moral absolute. Eventually, however, their movement grew like a river that overflows its banks; the motives became polluted. The abolitionists found themselves fighting alongside racists whose only goal was free land for white people, and they found themselves allied with people who hated the political power of the South more than they hated slavery. These mixed and impure motives troubled the abolitionists. Some quit the fight; others stayed the course.

Phyllis Schlafly, the contemporary activist who led the campaign against the ratification of the feminist Equal Rights Amendment in the 1970s, would have had good advice for these troubled abolitionists. She has said that on matters of motive she is very liberal. She is happy for anybody to support her goals for whatever reason they choose. Political success requires the building of coalitions, and whenever moral truth is caught in the grasp of politics, moral people must use the techniques of politics to remedy the problem. Coalition building is a basic strategy.

3. Abolition embraced strong rhetoric but tolerated baby steps. In the early years of the antislavery campaign, abolitionists insisted that slavery end immediately. But to many ordinary people, this just didn't make sense. They believed slavery was wrong, but they also thought that chaos would result if millions of untrained, illiterate people were suddenly set loose and required to survive on their own. Eventually, the "immediatists" listened, scaled back their rhetoric, and began to argue that abolition be "immediately begun" but gradually implemented.

That fact has implications for today. Leaders in the pro-life movement have begun to realize that there is nothing they can do to end all abortions at one time. The country isn't ready for it, and the courts won't allow it. Pro-life leaders have begun adjusting their sights to trim abortion back little by little: no federal funding, no abortions at military installations, parental consent and notification laws, women's "right to know" laws that require accurate information about the physical development of unborn children, and finally, more attention to health care and adoption options for needy pregnant women.

But the pro-life movement lost many years getting around to this strategy. In the first few years after the *Roe v. Wade* decision in 1973, the predominant belief was that since all human life was sacred and must be spared, anyone who stopped short of working for a total ban against abortion was somehow selling out.

The problem here is the same one that must be faced whenever government has codified immorality. Moral matters are absolutes, and people who hold moral beliefs believe deeply in them. Governance, however, is the art of compromise. When government, whether through neglect by good people or by tyranny, begins to rip away at the foundation of moral truth, that foundation will not be restored all at once. It must be restored painstakingly, stone by stone. The abolitionists, the "immediatists," eventually understood this. The pro-life movement has begun to figure this out in our day.

4. *Working in the system was essential.* The abolition movement quickly understood that because slavery was protected by unjust laws, slavery wouldn't be stopped unless government policy changed. That began to happen when the abolitionists stopped merely sending petitions to Congress and started sending abolitionists. When Congressman Joshua Giddings and his colleagues began working from inside of the political process, they shook the underpinnings of slavery and stood the national political party system on its head.

Sometimes Christian leaders warn believers away from participating in the process of government. For many reasons explained elsewhere in this book, that's unbiblical. It's also silly. Government policies play an extraordinary role in determining the moral tone of a nation. Many citizens believe things are right simply because they are legal. The law is an influential teacher of right and wrong, and it is the responsibility of citizens to make sure that laws are compatible with moral truth and are enforced. I suspect that many women seeking abortions believe they are right in doing so for no other reason than that abortions are legal. If that changed, many abortions would be stopped; women would assume that since abortion is not legal, it must not be right to get one.

5. *Christian virtues were essential.* The abolition movement grew from small beginnings to engulf the nation because some of the abolitionists had the patience and persistence to work within the system, starting from the ground up. Theodore Weld started in back-country churches, and difficult though it was, he won a hearing by his thorough understanding of the issue and his display of Christian virtues, particularly humility, kindness, and compassion for others. As the groundswell built in the hinterlands, it became possible to pressure the political system, then to infiltrate it, and finally to build a majority within it.

Weld was not the only significant abolitionist, of course. In fact, he was not even well known in the movement or among early historians of the movement. The most notable abolitionist of the day was William

Lloyd Garrison of Boston, whose tactics were far different than Weld's. Garrison was a fiery polemicist and editor of a prominent abolitionist newspaper called *The Liberator*. He aimed his punishing rhetoric at all opponents of immediatism. His blood-boiling editorials were circulated in the slave-owning South, where grand juries indicted him in absentia and politicians demanded that his paper be shut down.

The turmoil was noticed by northern newspapers, which found Garrison to make for colorful copy. He became a household name all around the country, a controversial and strident voice. Rather than patiently teach and kindly persuade, as Weld did, Garrison grew ever more vindictive, particularly against clergymen who disagreed with him. Garrison was disgusted by government, ecclesiastical as well as civil, and once said that only Jesus Christ was fit to run the country. He stayed aloof from politics, and he urged his followers to do the same.

For many years, historians credited Garrison with launching the abolition movement, because his name and his writings were so prominent. More recently, however, historians have begun giving more of the credit to the elusive Weld, who wrote so much that was unsigned or under a pseudonym. It is significant that the first groundswell of popular opinion against slavery grew in Ohio, where Weld spent so much of his time preaching and teaching, rather than Boston, the locus of Garrison's activity.

6. An unbalanced life breeds cynicism. Weld's great courage and determination earned him a hero's place in the annals of abolition. But his struggle often was not against the institution of slavery itself; rather, it was against the Christian churches whose leaders failed to speak out. Apparently this bred discouragement in him, and later in life he withdrew from active church involvement. He grew dissatisfied with organized worship, and he and his wife retreated into a much less formal mode of religion that centered on the teachings of Jesus but eventually degenerated into a kind of Unitarianism. More details about this part of his life are unknown because his biographer hasn't given us a clear picture.

What we do know, however, is that anyone who throws himself against an implacable moral foe needs to balance his activism with more gentle aspects of the Christian faith—with regular worship, with accountability to others, and perhaps with activities that occasionally take him well away from the rigors of battle. During the fight against slavery, Weld's friends urged him to do ever more, because he was so skillful at what he did. In a situation like this it is easy to burn out and grow spiritually cold. Whether this actually happened to Weld is speculation, but it seems reasonable.

The fact that Weld grew distant from the organized church cannot lessen the significance of what he accomplished for the church. His fearlessness, his humility, and his determination provide inspiration for us all, and his later life serves as a caution against engaging so relentlessly for such a long time without sufficient withdrawal and diversion.

APPENDIX A-2
One Mom Who Mattered

Communion always moved Harriet. On this particular Sunday, however, her thoughts were far from her Savior, the central figure in her life. Throughout the service, her meditation was jarred again and again by a horrible image that pounded in her head, one she would later say was sent by the Lord.

Indeed, a remarkably ugly picture had fixed itself in the mind of this soft-spoken wife and mother of six as she sat in church in the picturesque New England town of Brunswick, Maine. It was the image of a slave being beaten to death at the hand of his master, a man driven to fury not by any act of insolence or disobedience on the part of his slave but rather by the slave's serenity in the face of his master's raw hatred. The slave was dying a martyr's death, sustained, like Harriet, by his devotion to Jesus Christ.

The service was a blur to Harriet. When it ended, she gathered the children, took them home, and wrote out on paper what she had seen in her mind that morning in church. Harriet had written magazine articles before, but she had never attempted anything like this. What she wrote so shocked her that she put the pages away and didn't turn to them again. Some months later, in March of 1851, her husband, Calvin, discovered them. He read them and—moved to tears—brought them to his wife.

"Hattie," he said, "this is the climax of that story of slavery you promised sister Katey you would write. Begin at the beginning and work up to this, and you'll have your book." Thus was born *Uncle Tom's Cabin,* the novel that swept a nation to the brink of civil war.[1]

Harriet was the daughter of Lyman Beecher, the former seminary president and the best-known Presbyterian preacher of his day. Harriet's five brothers were clergymen as well. She was married to Calvin Stowe, an accomplished Bible scholar and seminary professor. Hers was a family fully devoted to the gospel.

Harriet would never have described herself as an abolitionist at that point in her life, but she had seen the ugliness of slavery and the raw emotions that the subject produced among men of culture and education. Years earlier, the Beecher family had been living in Cincinnati when her father was president of the fledgling Lane Theological Seminary. Cincinnati lay across the Ohio River from Kentucky, a slave state. Although slavery was illegal in Ohio, the businessmen of the bustling city depended upon the goods and the labor produced by the slave trade.

Harriet was angered when sons of well-to-do families in Cincinnati rioted and vandalized the printing press of James Birney, an Alabama gentleman and former slave owner who had converted to the cause of abolition and moved to Cincinnati to begin publishing an abolitionist newspaper. She was offended by the hypocrisy of learned people who knew what slavery was but turned a deaf ear to cries against it because the products of slave labor made them well-off. Harriet and her brother Henry Ward did what they could to help Birney and his assistant, Gamaliel Bailey, through the tense days. Hence the paper kept publishing. Although the newspaper would continue under Bailey, Birney left town for the lecture circuit and a broadened role in the abolitionist movement.

USING HER TALENT FOR THE CAUSE

That was 1836. Now, 14 years later, her husband had accepted a position as professor of religion at Bowdoin College in Maine. Harriet was thrust into a new arena where the battle over slavery would rage. Congress had just passed the Fugitive Slave Act, which required all citizens to aid in the return of any escaped slave, even those who had managed years earlier to free their shackles and build new lives in northern cities. Suddenly, furor over slavery surged around her again, even here in New England, where no black was now safe. Letters from her sister Katey in Boston brought news of long-established black families being torn apart by slave traders who kicked in doors in the middle of the night. The citizen backlash brought federal troops to keep the peace in Boston. Slavery! Even here in Maine this accursed issue would not leave Harriet alone.

So she resolved to contribute her talents to the cause of freedom. After a few false starts at writing an article about slavery, she had her strange vision in church, and she knew which direction her article would take. She contacted her old friend Gamaliel Bailey, who now was publishing an abolitionist newspaper in Washington, D.C., called the *National Era*. She described her article and cautioned him that it might run to three or four installments in his newspaper. Harriet wrote, "I have always felt that I had no particular call to meddle with this subject, and I dreaded to expose even my own mind to the full force of its exciting power. But I feel now that the time has come when even a woman or a child who can speak a word for freedom and humanity is bound to speak."[2]

The editor, Bailey, was courteous and encouraging. Thus began the strange publication of her novel, chapter by weekly chapter, in a newspaper. She grabbed what time she could in her busy household, an hour here, an hour there, clearing space at the kitchen table or spreading her papers in the study when Calvin wasn't using it. Her characters developed and her story took form as the weekly deadlines pressed in upon her. Harriet missed only one installment. This happened when one of her characters, little Evangeline, died. Harriet had not wanted it to happen, but she could see Eva's death approaching in her mind's eye. When she wrestled through that unhappy chapter, she was so overcome with grief (for Eva's death unleashed the pent-up sorrow from the death of one of Harriet's own babies) that she took to her bed and missed a week's production. Thousands of *National Era* readers were shocked when they opened their papers and didn't find the chapter.

It was the story's climax that most riveted the readers. The main character, Tom, was struck down under the hand of his evil owner, Simon Legree. But it was not so much the death of Tom that tugged at the hearts of Harriet's readers, who kept growing in number week by week; it was the way in which Tom died, in thorough possession of his faith in Christ, compassionate and forgiving of his tormentors until his last breath, secure in divine peace and human dignity.

This culminating scene occurs as Legree seeks to beat out of Tom his knowledge of the whereabouts of a runaway. Tom is unwilling to betray this slave, who, unlike himself, has not been able to withstand the injustice of bondage to the evil master. The passage is worth quoting at length:

> Legree drew in a long breath; and, suppressing his rage, took Tom by the arm, and, approaching his face almost to his, said, in a terrible voice, "Hark 'e, Tom!—ye think, 'cause I've let you off before, I don't mean what I say; but, this time, I've made up my mind, and counted the cost. You've always stood it out again' me: now, I'll conquer ye, or kill ye!—one or t' other. I'll count every drop of blood there is in you, and take 'em, one by one, till ye give up!"
>
> Tom looked up to his master, and answered, "Mas'r, if you was sick, or in trouble, or dying, and I could save ye, I'd give ye my heart's blood; and, if taking every drop of blood in this poor old body would save your precious soul, I'd give 'em freely, as the Lord gave his for me. O, Mas'r! don't bring this great sin on your soul! It will hurt you more than 't will me! Do the worst you can, my troubles'll be over soon; but, if ye don't repent, yours won't never end!"
>
> Like a strange snatch of heavenly music, heard in the lull of a tempest, this burst of feeling made a moment's blank pause. Legree stood aghast, and looked at Tom; and there was such a silence, that the tick of the old clock could be heard, measuring, with silent touch, the last moments of mercy and probation to that hardened heart.

It was but a moment. There was one hesitating pause,—one irresolute, relenting thrill,—and the spirit of evil came back, with seven-fold vehemence; and Legree, foaming with rage, smote his victim to the ground.

Scenes of blood and cruelty are shocking to our ear and heart. What man has nerve to do, man has not nerve to hear.... And yet, oh my country! these things are done under the shadow of thy laws! O, Christ! thy church sees them, almost in silence!

But, of old, there was One whose suffering changed an instrument of torture, degradation and shame, into a symbol of glory, honor, and immortal life; and, where His spirit is, neither degrading stripes, nor blood, nor insults, can make the Christian's last struggle less than glorious.

Was he alone, that long night, whose brave, loving spirit was bearing up, in that old shed, against buffeting and brutal stripes?

Nay! There stood by him ONE,—seen by him alone,— "like unto the Son of God."

The tempter stood by him, too,—blinded by furious, despotic will,—every moment pressing him to shun that agony by the betrayal of the innocent. But the brave, true heart was firm on the Eternal Rock. Like his Master, he knew that, if he saved others, himself he could not save; nor could utmost extremity wring from him words, save of prayers and holy trust.

"He's most gone, Mas'r," said Sambo, touched, in spite of himself, by the patience of his victim.

"Pay away, till he gives up! Give it to him!—give it to him!" shouted Legree. "I'll take every drop of blood he has, unless he confesses!"

Tom opened his eyes, and looked upon his master. "Ye poor miserable critter!" he said, "there ain't no more ye can do! I forgive ye, with all my soul!" and he fainted entirely away....

Yet Tom was not quite gone. His wondrous words and pious prayers had struck upon the hearts of the imbruted blacks, who had been the instruments of cruelty upon him; and, the instant Legree withdrew, they took him down, and, in their ignorance, sought to call him back to life,—as if *that* were any favor to him.

"Sartin, we's been doin' a drefful wicked thing!" said Sambo; "hopes Mas'r'll have to 'count for it, and not we."

They washed his wounds,—they provided a rude bed, of some refuse cotton, for him to lie down on; and one of them, stealing up to the house, begged a drink of brandy of Legree, pretending that he was tired, and wanted it for himself. He brought it back, and poured it down Tom's throat.

"O, Tom!" said Quimbo, "we's been awful wicked to ye!"

"I forgive ye, with all my heart!" said Tom, faintly.

"O, Tom! do tell us who is *Jesus,* anyhow?" said Sambo;— "Jesus, that's been a standin' by you so, all this night!—Who is he?"

The word roused the failing, fainting spirit. He poured forth a few energetic sentences of that wondrous One,—his life, his death, his everlasting presence, and power to save.

They wept,—both the two savage men.

"Why didn't I never hear this before?" said Sambo; "but I do believe!—I can't help it! Lord Jesus, have mercy on us!"

"Poor critters!" said Tom, "I'd be willing to bar' all I have, if it'll only bring ye to Christ! O, Lord! give me these two more souls, I pray!"

That prayer was answered![3]

After a few loose ends were tied up, the novel skidded to a finish. Thousands who had not previously understood the horror that slavery could become were melted by this work of fiction. Overnight, Harriet Beecher Stowe became a sensation. The publisher who offered to bring out the work in book form grew ever more dismayed as he saw the material grow, week by week, in the *National Era.* He wasn't at all certain he could sell his intended print run of 5,000 and had hoped for a slimmer volume to cut his losses. He also approached the Stowes about paying for half the costs of the printing in exchange for half the profits, but Harriet and Calvin were living on a meager college professor's salary and couldn't participate financially.

The publisher needn't have worried. The 5,000 books in the first print run were gone in two days. Twenty thousand sold in three weeks. In six months, sales totaled 100,000, and still there was no slackening in demand. The book was a huge success in Europe, and pirated editions, over which Harriet's publisher had no control, flooded the continent. Thousands upon thousands of people were moved by the tense drama of Tom's plight, and they rallied to the cause of abolition.

Scriptwriters adapted the book for the stage, and theatrical versions abounded. The stage plays, however, would prove unkind to the novel and its main character. In adapting the novel, writers shrunk the character of Uncle Tom. His Christian dignity in the face of raw evil faded, and he became a shuffling, bootlicking pushover to be manipulated by white bosses. It is this stage legacy, rather than the book character, that has made "Uncle Tom" a term of derision among African Americans today.

The character Tom died a martyr's death. It was his Christian conviction that would not allow him to betray his fellow runaway slave, and it was the peace of Christ in him that drove Legree to fury. Harriet painted her character in more vivid Christian colors by turning him into a Christ figure, since, at the moment of his death, Tom forgave his tormentors.

The faith that brought Tom through his ordeal was the same faith that led his author, Harriet, to strike her blow against slavery. It is a faith that helps one person to bear up under injustice and convicts another person to work for an end to injustice. Harriet was no wild-eyed radical. In fact, most of what she wrote through her productive years had nothing to do with slavery. What possessed her to write *Uncle Tom's Cabin* was simply her ability to see right and wrong, along with a conviction that she should use her talents to redress the evil she saw.

The conviction came from God. Her love of God was so pronounced that one of her biographers titled two chapters in his book with the words "The Daughter." He did this because he said she had two fathers, "a father in heaven as well as a father on earth, and her relationship to Him was the central fact of her life."[4]

We live in a time when many Christian leaders refuse to carry their faith beyond church, because they do not want to offend anyone by proclaiming God's word in the public square. For Harriet Beecher Stowe, this was never a question. She believed that because of her faith, she could not remain silent in the face of wrongdoing, and she resolved to put her talent to work in the cause of godly righteousness.

In 1862, with the Civil War on and President Abraham Lincoln on the verge of issuing his proclamation for the emancipation of slaves, Harriet journeyed to Washington, D.C., for a meeting with him. To Harriet, it was the culmination of everything the book stood for. Biographer Johanna Johnston tells the story:

> Charley [her son] was by her side as she entered the White House and was escorted to one of the small rooms that Lincoln used as a study. Small, neat, composed, her great eyes intent, she watched as an immensely tall figure unfolded itself from a chair, and stood and came toward her, the movements slow and a little awkward. The rest would be legend, forever after, to Harriet and all her family. Towering over her, Lincoln put out his great hand and took her small one in it.
>
> "So this is the little lady who made this big war?" he said.[5]

APPENDIX A-3
Making a Difference in Cincinnati—and Making It Last

When people act together, intelligently and sensibly, each contributing as he or she is able, the results can be astonishing. That's what happened when a few good citizens in Cincinnati decided to stand up to the country's most notorious purveyor of hard-core pornography, Larry Flynt.

No individual in America personifies sexual raunchiness more than Flynt. He is the publisher of *Hustler* magazine and other sexually explicit publications that depict women as sexual toys, that celebrate excrement, retching deviance, and weird sexual fetishes. For a while, until a court stepped in, a *Hustler* cartoon feature even made fun of child molesting.

Flynt is the kind of man whom the media love to lionize as a roguish defender of its own Holy Grail, the First Amendment. Flynt wages legal wars to extend the far perimeters of free speech, and that makes the mainstream media, camped well within the boundaries of the First Amendment, feel safer.

That's what makes Larry Flynt doubly frustrating. As a media hero, he escapes the derision that ought to be heaped upon him. In fact, Hollywood even blessed him with his own movie, *The People vs. Larry Flynt,* starring Woody Harrelson as Flynt, and directed by the left-wing promoter of revisionist reality, Oliver Stone.

In 1976, when Flynt was just breaking into the pornography business, he opened a pornographic bookstore in Cincinnati. But the local prosecutor, Simon Leis, was as tough as they come and promptly slapped obscenity charges against him. Flynt was convicted and spent five months in prison before a higher court overturned the conviction and ordered a retrial. Before that new trial took place, Flynt was shot in Georgia, paralyzed from the waist down and confined to a wheelchair for the rest of his life. Severe health complications over the next few years kept the trial from proceeding.

Flynt had seen enough of Cincinnati. He and his *Hustler* magazine kept their distance for the next 20 years. But then he came back for the local premiere of his movie and decided to take on the city again by opening a porn store in the middle of downtown.

It should have been easy. Times had changed. Flynt had not only his smart lawyers but also his Hollywood movie and media reputation working for him. In fact, nothing did happen for a few months after his new place opened. Then one day, a store clerk sold an obscene video to a minor. In response, on a colorful night of flashing police car lights and television news crews scurrying about, the police raided the store. A grand jury decorated Flynt with 15 counts of pandering obscenity and operating a sexually oriented business without a license. Flynt pleaded innocent, crowing that the trial would be his triumph over this town. More important, he wanted his victory to drive a stake through the outmoded idea that anything could be deemed obscene and therefore illegal.

But Flynt never got his glorious victory for the First Amendment. Only two days after the trial began in 1999, he surprised everyone by pleading guilty. In exchange for no jail time, he agreed never again to sell sexually explicit videos in Cincinnati. This turn of events stunned First Amendment experts all across the country. They couldn't imagine why Flynt would turn tail and run. But it wasn't so hard to figure out. While the commentators might have understood trends in First Amendment law, they didn't understand Cincinnati. Flynt evidently realized what they did not—that even after 20 years, attitudes in this town hadn't changed much and he couldn't win a trial against a jury box full of Cincinnati prudes.

CINCINNATI: IN A LEAGUE OF ITS OWN

When it comes to concepts like decency, Cincinnati is a place set apart. The city has an extraordinary history of tough prosecutors and effective grassroots activists. Cincinnati has no porn shops or strip bars. In fact, there isn't one within 25 miles of the city. For those who trade in the sex business, it's easier to make a buck on the back side of the moon than in this part of the country. Cincinnati is swimming against the current and doing quite nicely at it.

The legacy began in 1971 when the tough, honest, and very conservative Simon Leis was elected Hamilton County prosecutor. He had a novel idea: He decided to enforce all the laws, even the controversial ones like obscenity. So he began closing the town's strip bars and porno joints, including the adult bookstore opened by the newcomer Larry Flynt. A group of Christian people calling themselves Citizens for Decent Literature organized themselves to make sure that when Leis enforced the obscenity laws, he received a groundswell of approval from at least some of the citizens.

Even so, it was never easy, especially when Leis took on sexual explicitness that had slipped into mainstream art. When the stage play *Oh! Calcutta!* came to town, he went after it and was roasted in the local media. That criticism got to him. But one weekend, he and his wife went shopping. He tells what happened:

A fellow came up to me to congratulate me for the effort we made. He said, "Can I do anything for you?" He happened to be a Baptist minister. I said, "Yes, you can. You see the type of criticism I've been getting, and you've seen the type of letters the paper is publishing. How about going to your church on Sunday and getting some support for our side?" He not only went back to his congregation; he went to every Baptist church in town. All of a sudden there was an outpouring of support, and suddenly the criticism stopped.

Ultimately Leis didn't prevail against the play, but his willingness to take it on, and his successes against the sexually oriented businesses in town, began setting a high moral tone in the city.

A WILDCAT STRIKE FOR RIGHTEOUSNESS

In the 1980s that tone would be set in concrete. A Presbyterian minister, Jerry Kirk, had become anguished over the toll that pornography was taking on some of the men in his congregation, destroying marriages and family life. His torment led to lengthy prayer, and that led to the formation in 1983 of a new citizens group that would eventually be called Citizens for Community Values (CCV). Kirk passionately preached his convictions to other local pastors, and they joined the cause. Those church connections have become a lasting distinctive of CCV. Soon, Kirk went on to form a national antipornography organization, but locally the roots he planted with CCV began to take hold.

Campaigns began against the Playboy cable channel in town, against convenience markets that sold pornography, and on behalf of a display ordinance that would at least put porn magazines behind blinder racks. CCV taught volunteers how to picket stores that carried pornography and how to survey the contents of those stores to determine how bad the books, videos, and magazines were. Volunteers also learned how to make polite but firm complaints to local prosecutors and to praise them publicly when they took action.

One of those early volunteers was Phil Burress, a businessman who had been a truck driver in the late 1960s. In his previous work he'd displayed several qualities that would later make him successful in CCV.

One quality was a knack for dealing with people. During his trucking days, he proved to be a popular member of his truck drivers' union, and when it needed a candidate for chairman, he was a natural choice. He was surprised by the nomination but took on the challenge and won. It was a fiercely fought election, and the first thing he did after winning was to invite some of the people who campaigned against him to join his leadership committee. That united the factions in the union, and it grew in size and effectiveness. He was hired full-time by the union in 1971 and represented a six-state Midwestern region with 6,000 union employees in it.

Burress also had a consuming sense of righteousness. One day a young, attractive woman, one of his union members, came to him, obviously agitated but reluctant to talk. Burress coaxed her into describing her trouble. Her boss had propositioned her and threatened her with the loss of her job if she declined. Burress felt the blood rush to his head. He jumped up and stomped down the hallway to the executive's office. He burst in on a meeting the boss was having and slammed his fist down on the table. He demanded to know why bosses were propositioning women. All the men around the table reddened, and a couple left the room.

As it turned out, propositioning women was a normal occurrence, but the women were afraid to talk about it. That incident ended in a wildcat strike, with Burress shutting down the trucking company from Chicago to Atlanta, Pittsburgh to St. Louis. He was hauled into federal court over that, but when the company's attorneys heard the reason, they put the women on the stand. They testified, and the guilty managers were fired. The judge gave Burress a day to get his drivers back on the road.

"With me it was about right and wrong and justice," Burress said. "I never played favorites. On many occasions my people got caught sleeping on the job, and I had to represent them. I did my own investigation, and if the charges were true, I would show up at the hearing because I had to, but I wouldn't speak. I was asked, 'What do you have to say for your client?' I said, 'I don't have anything to say.' I wouldn't defend them."

Something else about Burress would help him in his fight against pornography. For 25 years he was a full-blown porno addict himself. He didn't fully throw it off until he became serious about his Christian faith and began talking about his problem. The Billy Graham organization printed his testimony in its *Decision* magazine, and he found himself making speeches everywhere. He was the butt of a few jokes after that, but he also received hundreds of phone calls from men who wanted to know how he'd broken free from pornography.

That firsthand familiarity with the corrosive lure of porn led Burress deeper into his association with CCV. He was hired in 1988 to be its strategic planner, and in 1991 he was named president of the organization. Doggedly, he has kept it on track over the years, training citizens to know where and what sort of pornography is available in their communities. They learn how to draw the community's attention to the problem, how to make complaints to the proper authorities, and how to congratulate them when they act. The organization emphasizes what it calls "the Power of One"—the idea that a single individual can make a difference in the community.

And that is the core reason for CCV's success. The organization has not only stable leadership but also a dedicated following. CCV has been able to inculcate in its many volunteers the vital notion that, acting one by one, they can contribute to a significant result for the whole community.

This core value was captured well by Dean Garbenis, CCV's director of research and training, when he told in the CCV newsletter what happened when one individual decided to take a stand:

> A businessman made his regular visit to his office supply store
> to purchase more computer disks. On this occasion, however,
> as he was standing in line to purchase the items, he noticed a
> mainstream magazine on the checkout periodical stand. The
> cover showed a completely nude woman from the navel up cov-
> ering her breast with one arm. He felt something explode in his
> heart—he knew he had to say something about the offensive
> magazine. He went to the front office and calmly asked to
> speak to the store manager.

As the store manager met him at the checkout lane, the businessman complimented the manager on the store's ability to meet his professional needs and on the wide selection of magazines. "But," he stated, as he picked up the offending magazine and placed it about an arm's length from the manager's nose, "this magazine is very offensive to me." The manager thanked him for his comments, took the magazine and went to the office.

As the businessman was outside, getting into his car, a woman quickly ran up to him. "Thank you, thank you," the excited woman exclaimed. "I watched you talk to the manager about that offensive magazine, and then I watched him go to the office and make a phone call.

"A minute later," she continued with an ear-to-ear smile, "he returned and removed *all* of those magazines! I have always wanted to say something when I saw offensive material but never had the courage because I didn't think it would make a difference. Now because of what I saw you do, it has encouraged me to speak up and not be afraid the next time I see something offensive."[1]

Little victories like this one are significant not only for their ability to build the confidence of volunteers but also for the way they help prosecutors win cases against such people as Larry Flynt. The magazine cover almost certainly wasn't obscene under the legal definition, but community standards are important in determining whether a particular publication is legally obscene. When CCV encourages people to speak up as this businessman did, they are contributing to a high community standard. This makes it more difficult for pornographers to argue in court that the community accepts their material.

MAINSTREAMING THE MESSAGE

With an agenda like this, one that prompts people to say something when offended by nudity and other pornographic images, it would have been easy for CCV to get itself ridiculed as a bunch of whining prudes who are trying to stamp out fun and the First Amendment. But that reputation didn't develop, and the reason it didn't is highly significant in understanding how Christian people can stand for righteousness without getting themselves sidelined.

First of all, over the years CCV decided that it should not be a Christian organization but rather a secular organization run by Christians. So it broadened its board of directors beyond pastors to business and professional laypeople in the community. Burress told me:

> In my mind, a Christian organization is a church. The problem is that people have turned their hearts away from the Lord and don't want to live by a moral standard. By thinking of ourselves as a secular organization, we move the debate from a moral argument to a harms argument. In our early newsletters we quoted a lot of Scripture. Then we thought, *Wait a minute. We're marginalizing ourselves. We really are not going to hit the mainstream if people perceive us as a Christian organization.* We decided to address the harms that people suffer when they don't live moral, upstanding lives.

In 1986 the Supreme Court issued a ruling called *Renton vs. Playtime Inc.* that acknowledged the harms associated with sexually oriented businesses. Such harms include prostitution, drug use, blight, and declining property values. When Burress speaks to the media or to political leaders, he talks about these issues rather than about moral values. He does not bring up censorship. "I always say that CCV is unalterably opposed to unauthorized censorship," he comments. "One can't be opposed to *all* censorship because then one would be in favor of slander and child pornography." The *Renton* decision gave him credible arguments that have helped to keep CCV in the mainstream.

Burress tries to anticipate attacks against his organization and blunt them before they do damage. A good example is a skirmish CCV had with the prosecutor in neighboring Butler County after he refused to enforce obscenity laws in his jurisdiction. CCV lobbied him hard and then publicly, but respectfully, criticized him for not doing his job. He responded in the media by blasting back at CCV.

To recover, the organization put on a conference for the Butler County community about guiding teens through the thicket of objectionable messages in popular media. The event was well advertised and cosponsored by leading citizens. The keynote speaker was former Attorney General Edwin Meese, who was in Cincinnati for another event and accepted Burress's invitation to stay over another day to address the conference. Nothing derogatory about the county prosecutor was said in response to his criticism of CCV, but the conference demonstrated that CCV was serious, real, and an upstanding presence in the area. Three hundred turned out for the event—a respectable showing for the size of the community.

On another occasion, CCV supported the Cincinnati prosecutor in seeking obscenity charges against the Cincinnati Art Museum when it scheduled a showing of the graphically sexual, homosexually themed photographs of Robert Mapplethorpe. That episode brought CCV criticism because this was no sleazy porno shop but one of the city's elite cultural institutions. In response, CCV launched a series of television ads, not about Mapplethorpe but about CCV's annual golf tournament. The spokesman on the commercials was Anthony Munoz, a member of the CCV advisory board and, as a Hall of Fame former player for the Cincinnati Bengals, one of the city's leading celebrities. The purpose of the commercials was not to recruit more golfers but to reinforce CCV's image as a mainstream organization. After all, extremists don't hold golf tournaments.

Incidentally, the obscenity charges against the art museum were dismissed, just as Flynt's obscenity conviction in 1977 was thrown out. But just as that experience kept Flynt out of Cincinnati for 20 years, so the art museum didn't bring in another sexually explicit art display after Mapplethorpe. Not only did the episode embroil it in undesirable controversy but in addition the museum paid $300,000 to defend itself against the charges—not something its donors appreciated.

Because of CCV's mission to speak out against indecency and pornography, it's an easy target for media critics. Burress explains:

The most natural thing your opponents are going to try to do is to destroy your credibility. If they can do that, then they can destroy your forum in the public square. Your credibility is more important than your army of volunteers. Your army is second, because you're not going to get an army behind you without credibility. Your credibility comes from the team around you, your advisory board, your board of directors.

Over the years, by carefully guarding its image and repairing it when it has been attacked, CCV has been able to recruit to its advisory board a stellar listing of locally prominent people. The board includes, in addition to Munoz, an Olympic gold medalist, two retired judges, the former Bengals head coach, the son of the owner of the Cincinnati Reds, the city's Catholic archbishop, its Greek Orthodox leader, and several prominent pastors and businesspeople.

They allow themselves to be identified with this antiporn organization because of its gentle, compassionate public persona. The organization was born with this attitude, and the pattern continues to this day. But it was given a stiff test in 1993, when CCV helped organize Issue 3, a citywide referendum that sought to overturn the City Council's granting of a special civil rights status to homosexuals.

FIGHTING THE ISSUES AND LOVING THE OPPONENTS

Burress said that during the Issue 3 campaign he was under tremendous pressure to run ads depicting homosexuals engaged in offensive antics. Plenty of this footage was available from gay pride parades on the West Coast. Burress refused to run the ads, believing them to be too inflammatory. Instead, CCV's most successful ad simply portrayed an African-American woman who said she was bewildered by people trying to compare what people do in a bedroom to someone's skin color. The ad, said Burress, conveyed the right message and it also built credibility for CCV.

Because it speaks out on two of the more controversial issues of the day, pornography and homosexuality, CCV risks fraying relationships with public leaders and philosophical opponents. Burress is constantly mending those relationships with striking success. He explained to me:

> One thing I was taught in the union was that my work was business, it wasn't personal. I don't think there is one person in Cincinnati who hates me or even dislikes me. Scott Greenwood, the ACLU attorney in Cincinnati, is homosexual, and even though we don't agree on anything, we sit down and we dialogue. We've debated each other but we treat each other with respect. When you go into a campaign like Issue 3, you realize that all of us are human beings.
>
> When I've gone into City Council to testify about hate crimes, people see me walk right up to the most liberal people in there and give them a hug, and that says a lot to the councilmen.

Burress's desire to be Christlike in his encounters with opponents served CCV well in 1995 when he proposed an idea that even his friends thought was crazy. An acquaintance in constitutional law, Gene McConnell, pointed out that Cincinnati had no ordinance prescribing zoning restrictions for sexually oriented businesses. Burress first thought it ludicrous for Cincinnati to need such an ordinance, because community pressure and the string of strong prosecutors had kept them out since 1978. Legal decisions since then, however, had made it clear that sex shops could not be banned completely if they were selling only material that was technically within the law. Sooner or later someone would open such a shop, take on the prosecutor, and win. In the new legal climate, the city must prescribe the rules for running such a business and zone those locations where they could operate. The rules could be tough, but there must be rules.

"They thought I was nuts," Burress recalls. "Even Si Leis." The idea that city fathers should provide zones for sexually oriented businesses in a tough town that had none and plainly wanted none seemed to make no sense. Finally Burress convinced a member of the city council, Phil Heimlich, that the city could be vulnerable, and Heimlich agreed to propose the ordinance. The process took years of dogged work. CCV made its arguments based on the threats to public safety brought on by these businesses, not on the morality issue.

The planning commission, realizing that this organization knew what it was talking about, brought its maps to the CCV office. Together, CCV and the city planners painstakingly began surveying the city, looking for areas where such businesses might locate with the least impact on schools, neighborhoods, and passersby. Every site they selected brought cries of protest from those living or working nearby, but eventually six zones were identified, and the City Council adopted the ordinance unanimously. Six months later, Larry Flynt rolled into town, and it was this zoning ordinance that tripped him up.

The unanimous 9–0 vote by the council was a stunning achievement for CCV. Although Cincinnati has a reputation as a conservative community, you wouldn't know that from the makeup of its city council. For most of the 1990s, the mayor—the leader of the council—was a pro-homosexual activist, and the majority on the council were political liberals. That's why the council had granted special civil rights status to the practice of homosexuality, the action overturned by Issue 3. The referendum, led by CCV, took place just prior to CCV's campaign for the zoning ordinance.

Councilman Heimlich underscored the effectiveness of CCV before the city council. "They testify effectively. They bring others along with them. It is very difficult for a politician to hear that kind of passion on an issue and then turn away from it. They know their facts. They do their homework.... Phil and Dean [Garbino, CCV's director of research and training] know more about sexually oriented business laws than half the lawyers in the country."

TURNING OUT THE CROWDS

But there is still another ingredient in effective advocacy work, something more than simply having the facts and conducting business in a Christ-like, friend-raising manner. It is the ability to mobilize people effectively. This gives political leaders the confidence that their courageous actions will be appreciated by the community and will be remembered at reelection time.

It is no easy task to get people to turn out for a civic function. In our day, people have more to do than ever before, with kids, careers, commutes, church on weekends, and Bible studies and small-group meetings during the week. More and more families need two adult wage earners to make ends meet. So even when they have time for outside functions, they seldom have the energy. Consequently it has become very difficult to produce crowds for any civic cause, and most local officeholders spend their time talking to tiny groups of people whenever they venture into the community.

In 1988, CCV held a citizens meeting to offer an opportunity for the county prosecutors in the Cincinnati region to explain to the residents what they were doing to enforce laws against pornography. The room was packed with more than 500 people—an astounding audience in the eyes of the prosecutors. One of them, Paul Twehues, summed up the thoughts of all the speakers that night: "I thought we'd get 20 or 30 people, and that would be a good crowd.... To us prosecutors, this [huge crowd] means 'keep on prosecuting those types of cases.' "

Burress says there is no magic formula in turning out a crowd, just a lot of common sense. Look at when CCV produced 300 for the event in Butler County, after the prosecutor took on the organization. In Burress's words:

> You just do your homework up front. We have a mailing list of
> 5,000 in Butler County. We've had a presence in that county
> for 16 years. We have a speaker's bureau. We have been in most
> of the churches. I have a voter registration list in my computer
> banks. I can take out a full-page ad, do whatever I have to do.
> We can create the event, as long as we don't go to the well too
> often. You can put people into a building if you have the right
> speaker. We had Ed Meese.

In working with volunteers, Burress is painfully realistic about the difference between good intentions and real help:

I may have 200 people who say they'll commit to writing letters, and I expect only a small percent of them actually to write one. But perception is important. I remember that our liberal Cincinnati mayor wouldn't meet with me, and I asked 200 people to write letters. About 75 of them did. In three days, the mayor called me and wanted to meet. Now those were the only 75 people in the entire Cincinnati area I could find to write a letter, but the councilman figured that if 75 people wrote him, a lot more must be thinking the same thing.

When we go into a church to do a Power of One seminar, every person in there might be called to a different thing. You just don't know what upsets them, and it is a lot of hard work to figure out what has motivated them. One might be upset by television programs, another by pornography, still another by Larry Flynt. We find out what it is that will keep their fire burning, and then we identify them in our database.

With its emphasis on "the Power of One," CCV celebrates small victories wherever they occur. One of its newsletters reported on a mom who complained to a manager about a racy magazine in a drugstore rack. The manager was not only polite but also appreciative. He removed the magazine. Another newsletter carried an account of a group that sat down with its county prosecutor to suggest that a video store might be carrying illegal videos. The prosecutor started an investigation.

Gina Bondick is one of those volunteers:

I'm a stay-at-home mom. I have three kids, and I've been a CCV volunteer for 14 years. This stuff wasn't part of my world. I started making phone calls to chain video stores to see if they had [pornography]. They said, "No, you have to go to our Kenton County store." That's my area. That made me mad. Just like a bird will chirp and squawk at you to protect her babies, why would I do any less?... People think because a video is on a shelf it must be legal, and they look the other way.

[CCV] gave me the tools to learn that what is popular is not always right, and what is right is not always popular.

Another CCV volunteer is Adrienne Green, now the head of her own organization that teaches children about the harms of our sexualized culture. She expresses well an important dimension of CCV's strategy, the fact that the work never ends. Vigilance must be constant:

You can never stop educating. There are always those people who, even though you've hit them with information 100,000 times, the very next time they say, "Oh, we have to do something about this." We have to continue to build awareness. You have to continue working. It's never ending. It takes volunteers. It takes caring, concerned, involved people.

GETTING POLITICAL

There is yet one more key to the success of CCV. People call Phil Burress frequently for advice on how to get rid of a strip bar or porn video store in their community. He advises them to speak to their prosecutor. When they tell him they've tried that but the prosecutor won't do anything, Burress's response is "Then you don't have a pornography problem; you have a political problem. Fix the political problem and you'll fix the pornography problem. When they say, 'I don't care about politics, I don't want to get involved in politics; it's pornography I hate,' then I say, 'I can't help you.' "

CCV and many organizations like it are established under section 501(c)(3) of the IRS tax code, which means that contributions to it are deductible from the donor's taxable income. This tax status allows the organization to engage in charitable and educational work for the public good, but it may not engage in supporting or opposing political candidates running for office. That, of course, is a roadblock because the political arena is often where these battles are fought. To solve the problem, Burress, like many leaders of such organizations, wears more than one hat.

Over the years, he has founded several political action committees (PACs): Family First, Equal Rights Not Special Rights, and American Families of Ohio. These organizations are permitted to contribute money to political campaigns and to endorse and oppose candidates for office. Money contributed to a PAC is not tax-deductible, and the accounting rules for keeping it separate from tax-deductible activities are strict.

By knowing the rules and attending to them scrupulously, Burress is free to switch hats from CCV to political activity, informing voters when a prosecutor running for election hasn't enforced the obscenity laws. His political action committees are also free to contribute money and endorse the candidates who will enforce the laws that are critical to CCV's work. Burress has found that there are people who readily understand the importance of involvement in political campaigns and are willing to donate to a PAC whose goals match their own. County prosecutors, who are so important to the success of CCV's mission, are much more likely to listen to the organization's concerns when they know it is backed up by an ability to help or hinder them when they run for reelection.

SUMMING UP

Michael Allen, the Hamilton County prosecutor who stood up to Larry Flynt and kept him from conquering Cincinnati, had this to say about the episode: "CCV has been an incredible help. I received numerous letters thanking us [for the Flynt prosecution]. That was something. In my job, I don't usually get thanked."

Remembering to send someone a thank-you note seems like a little thing. But to CCV, it's a big thing. And it is by concentrating on a few big things—and learning to do them well—that CCV has found success. Here are the elements in that success.

First, the organization has a clear focus, and that focus is pornography. CCV took on the Issue 3 homosexuality campaign only to show voters that the Council had turned politically leftward and to bring pressure on its members to act more conservatively. Conservative council members are less likely to support pornography.

Second, CCV understands the battlefield. It knows that most people don't share its moral distaste for indecency and pornography. It also knows that people *do* worry about crime going up and property values going down, which are the natural results of sex businesses. CCV preaches in the language that people understand. Here's another example. The CCV knows that the media will attack or ridicule any organization that seems to pose a threat to First Amendment freedom of speech. So CCV has avoided this pitfall by speaking out against censorship.

Third, it understands people. Because a pastor, Jerry Kirk, founded the organization and brought into it other key pastors who collectively shared a great burden for the people in their city, CCV has a culture that treats *all* people gently—its volunteers, its public officials, and its philosophical opponents. The second greatest commandment, to love one's neighbor as oneself, is evident in the daily life and public image of the organization.

Fourth, it understands the need for constancy. CCV plans to be a permanent force in the city. Its board of directors is strong, its budget is sound, and Burress knows he must be the CEO as well as the chief activist. Many organizations are born in the flurry of a worthy fight, but they die because they have focused all their attention on the issue that brought them into being. They have spent too little time on the vital matters of budgets, income, and strategic planning. Because activists too often don't pay enough attention to these more mundane matters, they find themselves strapped for money and burned out by a worthy cause.

Fifth, prayer is central. CCV has five task forces and nine support teams, but none is more important than its prayer support team.

Sixth, CCV constantly networks with like-minded organizations locally, statewide, and nationwide. Burress believes no one has all the answers, and for each problem there is someone who has been through it and is willing to share the experience. CCV constantly works in coalition with other organizations, occasionally keeping itself in the background. Some activist organizations are unwilling to do this, whether out of misplaced egos or the conviction that if a particular organization is not seen to be leading the charge, its donors won't contribute.

Barbara Black is a wife and mother of three in Kenton County,

Kentucky, part of the Greater Cincinnati area in which CCV is active. What upset her about pornography was the fact that wealthy men were in the business of exploiting women, and Barbara believed something had to be done about it. She waded in. Nine years later, sex businesses were gone from her community, and she was elected to the county commission. In looking back on her years of activism, she said, "I don't think the average citizen has any idea how much one can accomplish as an individual. If only more knew the power there is in just one person."

Unleashing that power has been the business of Citizens for Community Values since 1983, and what it has shown us is how that power can make community values fully consistent with moral values.

How to Get Started

ONE PERSON CAN DO A LOT.[1] STILL, no individual can do it all. So rather than tackling a social issue alone, you should help *your church* act corporately on issues facing your community. This biblical concept of calling affirms that our labors are best approached and accomplished by organized groups and associations. In other words, calling implies that work should be done in community for the community. And since the church is not an aggregate of individuals but a community of faith, members fulfill their individual callings for the benefit of the whole in accomplishing God's purposes. Each of us has a special calling of God for the edification of the entire body. We are dependent upon God and mutually interdependent upon each other. Simply put, we need to work together.

ORGANIZING FOR ACTION IN YOUR CHURCH

Many local churches in America have established impressive track records of effective social involvement. Protestant and Catholic, independent and mainline, these churches share a common conviction: The body of Christ must stand in the gap to provide moral influence in the public square. But they often share something else. Churches successfully engaged in social action have a committee devoted to this purpose as an official part of their ministry structure.

They are called by different names—social concerns committees, current issues councils, church and state or Christian citizenship committees—but their function is the same: to provide in-house leadership for congregational response to the social issues of the community. At Focus on the Family we call this kind of organized group a "community impact committee."

WHY A COMMITTEE?

People called to do business usually form or seek partnerships and corporations. Those who are called to the medical field set up or join practices and hospitals. Individuals who are called to humanitarian service establish or join nonprofit organizations. Scholars found or enter universities. Christians called to the foreign field either form or affiliate with mission agencies, and those called to support them organize or become members of missions committees in their churches. All these associations are people working together to serve society in their respective callings.

The idea behind establishing a community impact committee in your church is simply to get on with the social and political tasks that we are called to do as the people of God. Ideally, this committee is responsible for educating and equipping your church's membership toward effective social action.

WHERE DO I BEGIN?

The first five steps necessary to organize a community impact ministry in your church are as follows: (1) pray; (2) seek the affirmation and approval of church leadership; (3) recruit others who share your vision and calling; (4) draft a mission statement and organize for action; and (5) begin the flow of information. In the material that follows, we examine each of these steps. Finally, we offer an involvement continuum for cultivating others in your church to become better informed and more responsible citizens.

1. Pray.
Personal prayer is the first step in the development of your social vision and the establishment of a community impact committee in your church.

Because of the importance of prayer, it seems almost trite to devote only a few sentences to it here. Prayer is a central priority in the Christian life, and it is one that has no substitute. E. M. Bounds, a nineteenth-century authority on prayer, wrote:

> There can be no substitute, no rival for prayer; it stands alone as the great spiritual force, and this force must be imminent and acting.... It must be continuous and particular, always, everywhere, and in everything.... Many persons believe in the efficacy of prayer, but not many pray. Prayer is the easiest and hardest of all things; the simplest and the sublimest; the weakest and the most powerful; its results lie outside of human possibilities—they are limited only by the omnipotence of God.

Therefore, personal prayer must be the first priority as you work toward establishing a community impact committee in your church. Put first things first by taking this discipline seriously. There is no substitute for prayer.

Many people have a fundamental misunderstanding or misconception about the purpose of prayer. They believe that by petitioning God to "change things," God's will can, in effect, be brought into conformity with human desires. However, the true purpose of prayer is just the opposite. It is to bring our will into conformity with God's will. When our Lord said, "If you remain in me and my words remain in you, ask whatever you wish, and it will be given you," Jesus was not supplying a prescription for the manipulation of God. Instead, He was saying that by remaining in fellowship and being of one mind with Christ, our will would be brought into conformity with Christ's. In this relationship, our asking would be in accordance with God's desire.

In order to pray, you should prepare yourself through Bible study. Many people do not pray because they do not know how to pray. They think that prayer is a monologue uttered before God. Prayer is more correctly understood as a dialogue between God and the intercessor. If prayer is a dialogue, then God has something to say to you that He normally communicates through His written Word, the Bible. Therefore, we encourage you to prayerfully read the Bible, especially when it speaks to issues of social concern. By doing so, you prepare yourself not only to speak to God but also to listen to Him on these matters.

Personal Bible study equips you with things to pray about. It provides you with a knowledge of God's revealed will so you can talk with God about your relationship with Him in reference to His Word. We encourage you to converse with the Father and let your prayers arise out of what you have read. Andrew Murray said that prayer is to make a person "a partner with God." Consider that idea for a moment. We are to be God's partners as He extends His rule over the nations of the earth. This fact only underscores the importance of discerning and conforming to His will for our lives. Regarding prayer and your efforts to begin a community impact committee, Dr. Albert E. Day summarizes our thoughts:

> This can be said without presumption—that one who truly
> prays will have keener insight, will form sounder judgment, will
> evolve more intelligent plans, will achieve a greater mastery of
> situations, and will sustain more creative relationships with
> people than he ever would without prayer.

Just as prayer is essential to the establishment of a community impact committee, so is the affirmation and approval of your pastor and other church leaders.

2. Seek the affirmation and approval of church leadership.

This is the second step in starting a community impact committee in your church. Personal vision and commitment are not enough. The church must affirm and approve your plans for a community impact committee, and you must submit to their examination. Without this, most community impact committees fail.

Near the end of the apostle Paul's letter to the Romans, he extends personal greetings to several friends by name. One of these persons is Apelles, of whom he says, "Greet Apelles, tested and approved in Christ" (16:10).

Of Apelles we know next to nothing. However, his description of being "tested and approved" is relevant to our discussion. What exactly does this phrase mean? Who did the testing and approving? We believe the idea of being "tested and approved" is relevant to beginning a community impact committee. Part of the process involves being tested and approved in Christ.

How can this happen? The process is a function of the church leadership. If your calling is to social and political service, and if God has equipped you with the appropriate gifts, then the community of God's people should recognize and affirm you in this calling. Insight in this procedure can be gleaned from Paul's letter to Timothy. Paul exhorts Timothy, "Do not neglect your gift, which was given you through a prophetic message when the body of elders laid their hands on you" (1 Timothy 4:14). Though this passage refers specifically to Timothy's ordination to the gospel ministry, there is a principle here that applies to all callings within the Kingdom: Your spiritual overseers should recognize and affirm your calling and gift or gifts.

We encourage you to seek the counsel of your pastor or priest, elders, deacons, vestry, or the persons who are responsible for your spiritual oversight in determining your calling to social and political service. They see you in a different way than you see yourself, and this brings more objective spiritual knowledge and discernment into the process. The book of Proverbs is replete with exhortations to seek the advice of counselors. One particular proverb affirms the idea that the church is not an aggregate of individuals when it says, "The way of a fool seems right unto him, but a wise man listens to advice." Our advice is to seek the affirmation of fellow believers and of those charged with your spiritual oversight.

We also recommend that you meet with your leaders and review the contents of this book with them. It will help them to gain a clear understanding of your vision and direction. Their counsel and insight can be beneficial in these areas. Pray with them for God's direction in this matter and His blessing on your efforts.

This process of personal affirmation then extends to official approval for starting a community impact committee in your church. With the affirmation of your gifts and calling, and with the official approval to organize a committee, you are now ready to begin recruiting others.

3. Recruit others who share your vision and calling.

Let us emphasize that in one sense everyone has a calling to the basic responsibilities of citizenship (e.g., abiding by laws, paying taxes, voting intelligently, serving in the military). In another sense, however, social and political service is not for everyone. In fact, it probably will not be of interest to the majority of people in your church. If it were, who would be left to serve on the missions, evangelism, or worship committees? In forming a community impact committee, you are looking for "a few good men and women"—just like the Marine Corps. You are seeking those people in your church who share a similar calling and desire to be part of a group that will help other church members be better citizens. The net effects of meeting together will be mutual encouragement, shared vision, and increased guidance and direction.

The biblical concept of encouragement has been rediscovered in the modern business world. The idea is contained in the word *synergy.* Stephen Covey, one of today's most respected authorities on leadership and management, has popularized this word in his best-selling book *The Seven Habits of Highly Effective People.* The brilliance of Covey is demonstrated in his ability to take biblical concepts and popularize them in today's management lingo. Covey has masterfully accomplished this in his discussion of synergy.

What is synergy? "Simply defined, it means that the whole is greater than the sum of its parts," Covey writes. "It means that the relationship which the parts have to each other is a part in and of itself. It is not only a part, but the most catalytic, the most empowering, the most unifying and the most exciting part.... The essence of synergy is to value differences—to respect them, to build on strengths, to compensate for weaknesses."[2]

Synergy is nothing more than the biblical concept of encouragement repackaged for the modern mind. As helpful as Covey may be on this topic, a far more profound discussion of the idea is found in 1 Corinthians 12. You may want to take a few moments to read this passage. The New Testament writer of Hebrews also fully understood and communicated this idea of synergy when he said, "And let us consider how we may spur one another on toward love and good deeds. Let us not give up meeting together, as some are in the habit of doing, but *let us encourage one another*—and all the more as you see the Day approaching" (10:25, emphasis added). An understanding of synergy can even be found in the wisdom literature of the Old Testament: "As iron sharpens iron, so one man sharpens another" (Proverbs 27:17).

In meeting together with those who share your calling and vision, the synergy of these meetings will "spur" all of you "on toward love and good deeds." At your first meeting, let those in attendance share their burdens and interests relating to moral and social issues. In this way you will get to know something of the personal and common concerns of the group. Become apprised of the group's concerns for relevant community issues. Pray together about these matters, for each other, and for specific discernment, guidance, and direction about what to do. Then begin a study on biblical principles for social involvement.

In order to get started, you need to identify those persons in your church who have a social vision and invite them to pray and study in a fellowship group. You may already know who these people are, or you may have to go find them. One idea is to place an announcement in the church bulletin inviting any interested parties to a prayer meeting and study concerning social issues. Another idea may be to network within your Sunday school classes to identify others of like mind. After you have some people interested in meeting, set a time and place and get started.

These times together will provide the opportunity for a leader (or leaders) to surface. As the organization of your community impact committee evolves, the leadership requirements may be different from what characterizes the stereotypical "activist" in your church. Be sensitive to the need for servant-leaders who demonstrate a depth of spiritual maturity and respect within the church body. As you seek to determine who your leader will be, the qualifications for leadership found in 1 Timothy 3:2-12 and Titus 1:6-9 provide a rubric for candidate screening and selection. Persons of this character and maturity will have the wisdom, respect, and credibility to help make your committee a success.

4. Draft a mission statement and organize for action.

The organization of your community impact committee will be determined by three factors: mission, tasks to be accomplished, and available human resources. Mission is like a charter because it sets the committee's future direction and establishes a basis for organizational decision making. All planning, goals, and objectives should be tested in relation to the mission statement, because a mission statement is your committee's reason for existence. Organizational tasks and structure should be examined to determine how they serve the committee's mission.

The formulation of your mission statement involves a clear understanding of your purpose within the church and surrounding community. You must determine exactly what kind of "business" it is you plan to be in. As a church committee, your mission statement should be more focused than that of the church, but it should be derived from the church's mission. In formulating this statement, four primary questions should be answered.

First, what function or functions will the committee perform? They may include any or all of the following: (a) prayer concerts for government leaders and officials, policies, international peace initiatives, etc.; (b) citizenship education and the dissemination of information relevant to moral and social issues; and (c) effective political activism and social advocacy on our neighbors' behalf in the interests of love, mercy, truth, and justice.

Second, for whom will the committee function? The church membership, its leadership, or someone else?

Third, what actions or activities will the committee conduct to fulfill its functions?

Finally, why will the committee exist? For what purpose or end?

The process of working through these questions can be difficult and time consuming, but the process will be as valuable to your group as the final product itself. By wrestling with the "what," "who," "how," and "why" questions, the committee will be able to assess personal, group, and church values relative to social and political involvement. This exercise will provide even more insight on the tasks that you initially will need to undertake. Additionally, each member of your group will develop a sense of ownership in the committee's vision.

Here is a sample mission statement:

The community impact committee exists to serve this church
by helping to disciple its membership toward a fuller expression
of Christian faith in the public square. In this effort, the committee endeavors to foster the biblical virtues of love, mercy,
truth, and justice on our neighbors' behalf through prayer, citizenship education, and organized social action within local,
state, national, and international communities.

Once you have formulated the mission statement, you'll need to
determine the tasks necessary to accomplish your stated mission. You
will want to spell out in some detail the paths by which you intend to
accomplish your mission. What are the future "impacts" that you would
like to make in your community, and what are the sequential steps necessary to achieve these goals? Who will be responsible for these steps?

Your committee's organization will be finally determined both by the
number of people available to serve and the talents and abilities they
bring to the group. In a small church, the committee may be only a
handful of people, but in a larger church your committee could number
in the dozens. If your committee is small, it is probably unrealistic for
you to effectively engage 15 pressing social issues in your community. It
is possible that one or two issues will strain your committee's human
resources. In this situation, you will need to distinguish between what is
important and what is crucial for your church and community. What
can you do effectively with the resources God has given you? Once you
have determined these things, organize accordingly.

On the other hand, if you are part of a 50-member community
impact committee in a church of 3,000 members, then you can address
several opportunities. Parents and teachers could work on education
issues, attorneys on religious liberty and church-state issues, physicians
and nurses on human life and health care issues, etc. The possibilities are
endless, depending on the composition of your committee. The availa-
bility of someone with desktop publishing skills may help you develop a
newsletter, bulletin inserts, information sheets, and more. Someone with

the talent for persuasive writing may open an avenue for influencing public opinion in the editorial section of your newspaper. People who like to bake or make crafts could be involved in coordinating a bake sale or bazaar as a fund-raiser for the local crisis pregnancy center, soup kitchen, prison ministry, etc. Again, the sky's the limit.

A final consideration in the organization of your committee is the government of your church. What are the local requirements for leadership and organization of standing committees in your church? Some churches constitutionally stipulate that a pastor, elder, deacon, vestry member, etc., serve as a member of all standing committees. Be sure to investigate your church policy requirements in such cases to ensure that your committee complies with church order.

5. Begin the flow of information.

Solid education should undergird the actions of every community impact committee and must be an important function of your mission. Effective education is crucial in building a consensus within the church regarding social and political involvement. Furthermore, the dissemination of timely, accurate, and pertinent information on moral and social issues is a prerequisite to informed and responsible activism. Addressing the "why," "what," and "how" questions of social and political involvement must be a priority.

Busyness is pandemic in our culture. Most people just cannot find the time to stay informed. Pastors are often overworked and far too busy to keep up with every social issue. In this area, your community impact committee can be extremely valuable. By supplying leadership with the information to direct the congregation in matters of social and political involvement, you provide a much-needed service. Reliable information will win both the gratitude and the confidence of your church's leadership, better equipping your church for action. This increased confidence can only enhance the efforts of your committee. You would do well to consider the church leadership your primary constituency. The best service you can render the church is to serve them.

Church members may not be socially and politically involved simply because they do not have the time. Save them time by providing well-prepared, accurate information and analysis. For example, a handy-sized voter's guide on the local school board candidates would be a valuable digest of information that the average voter may not otherwise be able to get without great effort. In simple ways like this, you can serve the membership too.

Your church probably has a standing committee devoted to missions or evangelism. Most likely, the purpose of this committee is to help church members fulfill their responsibilities to the Great Commission. A community impact committee shares a similar role by helping church members fulfill their responsibilities as disciples and citizens in the public square. Your committee's mission augments and supports the ministry of your church and pastoral staff by helping teach the congregation about the Christian's role in society. In this manner you contribute to the overall effort of making disciples.

Your committee will need to read and study the issues. Continue your own education by subscribing to some informative periodicals. We recommend Focus on the Family's *Citizen,* a monthly magazine covering a broad range of social issues and providing a wealth of information and analysis. As an excellent alternative to the major newsweeklies, *World* is a newsmagazine that covers national and international events from a Christian viewpoint. Also, *First Things* is a monthly "thinking" journal that will supply substantive insight on issues relating to religion and public life. For a daily report on the hottest public policy issues facing Christians and how your committee can impact those issues, subscribe to Focus on the Family's Citizenlink e-mail update (www.citizenlink.org). The Citizenlink Web site has a host of other suggestions for pertinent reading on public policy issues. We also want to encourage you to tune in to *Family News in Focus,* a public policy broadcast of Focus on the Family that brings listeners up-to-the-minute reports on moral and social issues relating to the family. Visit the Citizenlink Web site for information on program schedules.

Maintain a reading schedule of good books pertinent to social and political involvement, and encourage "issue expertise" within your group. Each of you will have special interests. Cultivate these interests by reading and studying books, articles, and background papers in the areas of concern. Someone in your group may be concerned about educational reform or interested in the abortion issue. Yet another may be burdened for AIDS victims or concerned about homelessness, poverty, and welfare policy issues. Think of the potential areas of involvement for your committee that are represented by the broad scope of interests and concerns in your group. Fan these sparks of interest until they become a bonfire of social engagement and involvement. You need neither a large budget nor a staff of researchers to stay informed, since there are many organizations with full-time staff to do just that for you. Contact these organizations and build on their publications and networks. Most of their newsletters are relatively inexpensive or free. Here again, the Citizenlink Web site has suggestions for you.

Effective action on social and political issues is predicated upon knowledge coupled with insight and understanding. By staying informed and meeting with others who share your concerns, you will gain a deeper commitment to the cause and develop keener insight and understanding. All of these qualities will enhance your efforts at principled persuasion in the public square.

THE SOCIAL INVOLVEMENT CONTINUUM

Now that we have established the five steps to beginning a community impact committee, we would like to provide you with a five-phased model strategy for cultivating social and political involvement in your church. These principles, if properly applied, will help you foster and develop an increased consciousness, involvement, and vision for the culture in which we live. Specifically, this is a model strategy for motivating people in your church who have little or no interest in moral and social issues. It will encourage them to become more informed, involved, and responsible citizens. If we are serious about reclaiming the culture from the prevailing secularism, relativism, and individualism, greater numbers of Christians will need to be involved in a principled and persuasive way. One of the greatest challenges of a community impact committee will be to move Christians from no action to proaction. The social involvement continuum is a strategy to accomplish this.

The social involvement continuum can be summarized as the "Five I's of Community Impact." Briefly, they are identification, information, interest, involvement, and investment.

Identification. This phase concerns the process of identifying those you want to become more socially and politically involved. What worship services and programs do they attend? Are they young people, baby busters, baby boomers, empty nesters, or seniors? What are their social concerns relating to family, community, national, and international life? These types of questions will help you better inform them about the issues and concerns they care about and reach them with the appropriate media. You must begin informing them, and this leads to our next point.

Information. Once you have identified your target audience, you must provide them with information. Disseminate facts about the social and moral issues of concern to them. Then broaden that information to the spectrum of issues relating to justice in the public square. Where the people "are" will help to determine the media you use. Are they in the morning worship service(s)? Use bulletin inserts. Are they in the fellowship hall between Sunday school and worship hours? Set up an information table with newsletter and issue briefs. Do they use the church library? Stock it with books on social and political involvement as well as the periodicals we recommend. Do you have their mailing address? Create a newsletter or piggyback the church newsletter with a supplement. Do they attend adult Christian education classes? Seek to offer a course on Christian involvement. Find every creative and tasteful way to get the information out.

Interest. If you are providing relevant, accurate, and reliable information in a format of professional quality, people's interests will be piqued. When you touch people with information that affects their lives, you will have an opportunity to move them to some level of action or involvement.

Involvement is critical because it moves one from passive to active participation. Recruit involvement on the basis of information disseminated and interest created. At this point, you do well to solicit it personally—face to face.

"Bob, I'm going to the school board meeting on Tuesday night, and your presence would be an encouragement to me and the other parents concerned about the new curriculum. Would you be able to join us?"

"Sue and Bill, we'd love to have you come over for dinner next Sunday after worship services. Following dinner, our family will be participating in the Life Chain on Main Street, and we thought it would be a lot of fun for our families to do this together. Will you join us?"

"Cliff, three or four of us are meeting with the police commissioner to address our concerns about teen violence and to brainstorm what we can do as a church to help keep kids off the streets. I'd like you to be a part of this meeting. Would you be willing to join us?"

"Sally, a number of us are attending the town council meeting next Thursday to express our opposition to the proposed domestic partnership ordinance. Would you be willing to come with us?"

"George, we're organizing a work day to clean up and repair the city mission two weeks from Saturday. We could greatly use your help. In fact, the whole family is welcome to pitch in. Are you available to join us?"

Even after recruiting the people you've identified, they are probably not ready to make long-term commitments. Begin by soliciting simple one-time commitments that they will find satisfying. Make them as fun, positive, and enjoyable as you can. You can do this by organizing the involvement around other group activities. Follow up the social/political activity with a pizza party, coffee and dessert, or family get-together. Remember the discussion about "synergy." No one likes to do things alone. Look for things to do together that will provide meaning and significance. These involvement experiences will then lead to longer and deeper commitments or "investments."

Investment reflects the highest degree of commitment to the cause, because there is a willingness to contribute one's time, talents, and treasure. At this point, people are asking to be involved, joining the community impact committee, leading a march for life, organizing a voter registration drive, contributing financially to the cause they so deeply care about, and asking others to do the same. This level of commitment, however, has to be cultivated. It doesn't happen overnight. A common mistake of many community impact committees is to move from the identification phase to the investment phase by skipping all the important cultivation processes in between. This shortcut leads to frustration and discouragement. Cultivating social involvement takes a long time, and we encourage you to be patient. Gear up for the long haul. If you follow the social involvement continuum, we are confident you will see increased social and political consciousness, vision, and involvement in your church.

ACTION

Opportunities for social action are limited only by your imagination. As you study the issues and monitor current events, network with profamily groups, and seek the Lord's direction, you will find no shortage of things to do. Prioritize them! Always seek to maintain a balance between education and action. Action without proper education will be misguided; education without opportunities for action will prove unfruitful.

The following material constitutes a list of possible activities through which your committee can bring a positive influence to a wide range of social and political issues. This list is not exhaustive; there are many issues we have not mentioned here. It is simply a sampling of what other committees have done. Consult www.citizenlink.org for resources pertaining to the various issues.

ELECTIONS

The barest minimum for every citizen is to vote intelligently and regularly. But there is much more you can do to help elect qualified public servants in the interest of truth and justice.

- Conduct a nonpartisan voter registration drive at church. This is legal. Contact your local registrar of voters for further information.
- Distribute voter's guides.
- Host a candidate forum.
- Join a local party committee; become a delegate or precinct chairman.
- Volunteer to serve on a campaign.

- Run for office.
- Monitor local judges and their decisions, keeping in mind that many of these jurists face reelection contests. Be sure to hold them accountable.

ELECTED OFFICIALS

Supporting our governing officials and keeping them accountable are crucial tasks for the responsible citizen. Write a letter to your city, state, or federal representatives about legislation or issues affecting traditional values and religious liberty.

- Host a monthly "letter-writing night" to encourage and equip others to write as well.
- Establish a telephone tree in your church for mobilizing public opinion.
- Visit your officials in order to establish good relations; communicate your concerns.

SCHOOLS

Service is the key to local school involvement. You will be far more persuasive if your first contact with the school is unrelated to political controversy. Become known as a servant-leader within the school district. By volunteering to serve, you will earn the right to be heard when controversial topics arise.

- Volunteer to tutor, serve as a classroom aide, do a fund-raiser, or sit on a parents' advisory or textbook review committee.
- Start a Moms in Touch group to pray for your child's school.
- Attend school board meetings.
- Run for school board or support the candidate of your choice.
- Acquaint your local school board with quality sex education curricula that emphasize abstinence.
- Donate profamily books to your school library.

MEDIA

There are many ways to influence the quality of the media and entertainment industry.

- Write letters to the editor of your local paper and equip others to do so.
- Volunteer to serve on the citizen's committee that governs cable TV in your community.
- Write both local and national networks in support of good programs and in opposition to poor ones.
- Write the sponsors as well.
- Help to promote boycotts of the worst offenders.
- Write the FCC to alert them regarding inappropriate radio or television programming. Make sure you have accurate information (date, time, station, title of program, and specific examples of the content).
- Find out if your local telephone company has dropped its dial-a-porn services. If not, start a campaign against dial-a-porn.
- Call local radio shows to contend for traditional values in an articulate, informed manner.

Notes

Chapter 1

1. Tom Hess, "Uprising in Vermont," *Focus on the Family Citizen,* Dec. 2000/Jan. 2001, p. 36.
2. Ibid., p. 37.
3. Paul Smith, "Mothers Fight a Sleazy Teen Magazine," *Focus on the Family Citizen,* July 1988, p. 4.
4. Quoted in Tom Minnery, "So Long, *Sassy,*" *Focus on the Family Citizen,* May 26, 1997, p. 6.

Chapter 2

1. Kenneth Scott Latourette, *History of the Expansion of Christianity,* vol. 7 (Eyre and Spottswoode, 1945), pp. 503-4; quoted in John Stott, *Decisive Issues Facing Christians Today* (Old Tappan, N.J.: Fleming H. Revell, 1984), pp. 64-65.
2. William Barclay, *The Letters to the Galatians and Ephesians* (Philadelphia: The Westminster Press, 1976), p. 176.
3. Frank S. Mead, *The March of Eleven Men* (New York: Grosset & Dunlap, Inc., 1931), p. 74.
4. Philip Schaff, *History of the Christian Church,* 5th ed., vol. 3 (Grand Rapids: Wm. B. Eerdmans Publishing Co., 1910), p. 121.
5. Mead, pp. 81-82.
6. Mead, p. 96.

Chapter 3

1. Anonymous, *John Wesley the Methodist* (New York: The Methodist Book Concern, 1903), online at http://wesley.nnu.edu/methodist, no page number cited in online version.
2. Ibid.
3. J. W. Bready, *England: Before and After Wesley* (London: Hoddard & Stoughton, 1939), p. 192.
4. Ibid., p. 297.

5. Quoted in Bready, p. 252.

6. Bready, p. 177.

7. Bready, p. 178.

8. Bready, p. 178.

9. Bready, p. 178.

10. Richard Collier, *The General Next to God* (London: Collins, 1965), pp. 23-25.

11. Collier's fascinating biography provides the facts in this section about the early history of Booth's movement.

12. Collier, p. 194.

13. Collier, p. 194.

14. Collier, p. 104.

15. Collier, pp. 105-6.

Chapter 4

1. This illustration is adapted from an article by the author that appeared in *Christianity Today*, April 8, 1983, p. 34.

2. Lausanne Occasional Papers: No. 21 Grand Rapids Report: Evangelism and Social Responsibility: An Evangelical Commitment (Wheaton, Ill.: Lausanne Committee for World Evangelization/ World Evangelical Fellowship, 1982), p. 23; quoted in Alan Crippen, ed., *Reclaiming the Culture* (Colorado Springs: Focus on the Family, 1996), pp. 72-73.

3. Ibid., pp. 72-73.

4. Ibid., p. 75.

5. Billy Graham, "A Time for Moral Courage," *Reader's Digest,* July 1962, p. 49.

6. Ibid., p. 51.

Chapter 5

1. United States Census data, quoted in *USA Today,* July 19, 2000, p. 8A.

Chapter 6

1. William Barclay, *The Gospel of Matthew,* vol. 1 (Philadelphia: The Westminster Press, 1975), p. 100.

2. John R. W. Stott, *The Message of the Sermon on the Mount (Matthew 5-7)* (Downers Grove: InterVarsity Press, 1978), pp. 66-67.

3. Examples like this appear among the finest Bible commentators. See D. A. Carson, *The Sermon on the Mount* (Grand Rapids: Baker Book House, 1978), p. 27; Martin Lloyd-Jones, *Studies in the Sermon on the Mount,* vol. 1 (Grand Rapids: Wm. B. Eerdmans Publishing Co., 1959), p. 155; William Hendrickson, *The Gospel of Matthew* (Grand Rapids: Baker Book House, 1973), p. 282.

4. Associated Press, Oct. 17, 1996, reported in a column by George Will, *Washington Post,* Nov. 24, 1996, p. C7.

5. Hadley Arkes, "Right to Choose, or License to Kill," *The Weekly Standard,* Nov. 15, 1999, pp. 17-18.

6. Ibid., p. 18.

Chapter 7

1. John Stott, *Decisive Issues Facing Christians Today* (Old Tappan, N.J.: Fleming H. Revell Co., 1984), p. 15.

2. Michael J. Behe, *Darwin's Black Box* (New York: The Free Press, 1996).

3. Albert M. Wolters, *Creation Regained: Biblical Basis for a Reformational World View* (Grand Rapids: William B. Eerdmans Publishing Co., 1985), p. 17.

4. Ibid., p. 22.

5. George Washington, April 30, 1789, *A Compilation of the Messages and Papers of the Presidents* (New York: Bureau of National Literature, Inc., 1897), I:45; quoted in Alan Crippen, ed., *Reclaiming the Culture* (Colorado Springs: Focus on the Family, 1996), p. 27.

6. John Adams, *The Works of John Adams, Second President of the United States,* Charles Francis Adams, ed. (Boston: Little, Brown, 1854), IX:636; quoted in Crippen, p. 28.

7. C. S. Lewis, *Mere Christianity* (New York: MacMillan Publishing Co., 1943), p. 17.

8. Ibid., p. 19.

9. Wolters, p. 38.

Chapter 8

1. Spiros Zodhiates, ed., *The Complete Word Study Dictionary* (Chattanooga: AMG Publishers, 1992), pp. 106, 880-2.
2. Stott, *Decisive Issues,* p. 21.

Chapter 9

1. Cal Thomas and Ed Dobson, *Blinded by Might* (Grand Rapids: Zondervan Publishing House, 1999), p. 70.
2. Ibid., p. 147.
3. Ibid., p. 111.
4. Ibid., p. 91.
5. Ibid., p. 90.
6. Ibid., p. 135.
7. Ibid., p. 173.
8. Ibid., p. 177.
9. Ibid., p. 120.
10. John MacArthur, *Why Government Can't Save You* (Nashville: Word Publishing, 2000), p. 130.
11. Ibid., pp. 6-7.
12. Ibid., p. 21.
13. Ibid., p. 88.
14. Ibid., p. 12.
15. Ibid., p. 8.
16. Stephen Carter, *God's Name in Vain: The Wrongs and Rights of Religion in Politics* (New York: Basic, 2000), p. 7.

Chapter 10

1. Eugene H. Peterson, *The Message* (Colorado Springs: NavPress, 1993), p. 398.
2. *Word Study Dictionary,* p. 1208.
3. Reginald Coupland, *Wilberforce, A Narrative* (Oxford: Clarendon Press, 1923), p. 39.
4. Source unknown.
5. Coupland, p. 141.
6. Coupland, p. 141.

7. Originally quoted by the author in *Focus on the Family Citizen,* February 1999, p. 22, from which this section has been adapted.
8. John Wesley's Journal for September 16, 1743, quoted in J. W. Bready, *England: Before and After Wesley* (London: Hoddard & Stoughton, 1939), p. 210.
9. Ibid., p. 211.

Chapter 11
1. Quoted in Robert Jamieson, A. R. Fausset, and David Brown, *A Commentary, Critical, Experimental, and Practical, on the Old and New Testaments* (Grand Rapids: Wm. B. Eerdmans Publishing Co., 1973), vol. 3, p. 542.
2. Jeff Hooten, "Living Proof," *Focus on the Family Citizen,* October 1998, p. 21.
3. Deborah Mendenhall, "Nightmarish Textbooks Await Your Kids," *Focus on the Family Citizen,* Sept. 17, 1990, p. 6.

Appendix A-1
1. William W. Sweet, *The Story of Religion in America* (Grand Rapids: Baker Book House, 1973), p. 11.
2. Benjamin P. Thomas, *Theodore Weld, Crusader for Freedom* (New Brunswick: Rutgers University Press, 1950), p. 35.
3. Dwight L. Dumond, *Antislavery Origins of the Civil War in the United States* (Ann Arbor: University of Michigan Press, 1939), p. 28.
4. Thomas, *Theodore Weld,* p. 73.
5. The folly of colonization was proven by the numbers. The figure of two million slaves was the estimate in 1830, and the number was growing by half a million every 10 years. The American Colonization Society was founded in 1816 and in 20 years had sent fewer than 4,000 blacks to Liberia. Dumond, p. 11.
6. Ibid., p. 67.
7. Ibid., p. 40.
8. Gilbert H. Barnes, *The Anti-Slavery Impulse* (New York: Harcourt, Brace & World, Inc., 1933), p. 81.
9. Ibid., p. 81.

10. Thomas, *Theodore Weld,* p. 98.
11. James H. Fairchild, *Oberlin: Its Origins, Progress and Results* (Oberlin: Shankland and Harman, 1860), pp. 18, 26; quoted in Thomas, *Theodore Weld,* p. 98.
12. Barnes, *Impulse,* p. 85.
13. Ibid., pp. 85-86.
14. Ibid., p. 105.
15. Thomas, *Theodore Weld,* p. 130.
16. The Missouri Compromise of 1820.
17. J. W. Schuckers, *The Life and Public Services of Salmon Portland Chase* (New York: D. Appleton and Co., 1874), p. 147.

Appendix A-2
1. Johanna Johnston, *Runaway to Heaven* (New York: Doubleday, 1963), p. 203.
2. Ibid., pp. 203-4.
3. Harriet Beecher Stowe, *Uncle Tom's Cabin,* Signet Classic (New York: Penguin Putnam, 1966), pp. 446-8.
4. Edward Wagenknecht, *Harriet Beecher Stowe* (New York: Oxford University Press, 1965), p. 195.
5. Johnston, p. 357.

Appendix A-3
1. Dean Garbenis, "The Power of One," *Citizens' Courier,* winter 2000, p. 11.

Appendix B
1. Adapted from *Community Impact Handbook* by Alan Crippen II, with John Eldredge and Ron Reno. A resource of Focus on the Family.
2. Stephen Covey, *The Seven Habits of Highly Effective People* (New York: Fireside, 1990), pp. 262-263.

BIBLIOGRAPHY

Books

Ahlstrom, Sydney E. *A Religious History of the American People*, vols. 1 and 2. New York: Doubleday, 1975.

Ayling, Stanley. *John Wesley*. Nashville: Abingdon, 1979.

Barclay, William. *The Gospel of Matthew*, vol. 1. Philadelphia: Westminster, 1975.

Barclay, William. *The Letters to the Galatians and Ephesians*. Philadelphia: Westminster, 1976.

Barnes, Gilbert H. *The Anti-Slavery Impulse*. New York: Harcourt, Brace & World, 1933.

Batchelor, John C. *"Ain't You Glad You Joined the Republicans?"* New York: Henry Holt and Co., 1996.

Behe, Michael J. *Darwin's Black Box*. New York: Free Press, 1996.

Bready, J. W. *England: Before and After Wesley*. London: Hodder & Stoughton, 1939.

Carson, D. A. *The Sermon on the Mount*. Grand Rapids, Mich.: Baker, 1978.

Carter, Stephen. *God's Name in Vain: The Wrongs and Rights of Religion in Politics*. New York: Basic, 2000.

Collier, Richard. *The General Next to God*. London: Collins, 1965.

Cotham, Perry C., ed. *Christian Social Ethics*. Grand Rapids, Mich.: Baker, 1979.

Coupland, Reginald. *Wilberforce, A Narrative*. Oxford: Clarendon, 1923.

Cranfield, C. E. B. *Romans: A Shorter Commentary*. Grand Rapids, Mich.: Eerdmans, 1985.

Crippen, Alan, ed. *Reclaiming the Culture*. Colorado Springs, Colo.: Focus on the Family, 1996.

Dumond, Dwight L. *Antislavery Origins of the Civil War in the United States*. Ann Arbor: University of Michigan Press, 1939.

Eidsmoe, John. *God and Caesar: Christian Faith and Political Action*. Westchester, Ill.: Crossway, 1984.

Fairchild, James H. *Oberlin: Its Origins, Progress and Results.* Oberlin, Ohio: Shankland & Harman, 1860.

Graham, Billy. *A Biblical Standard for Evangelists.* Minneapolis: World-wide, 1984.

Hendrickson, William. *The Gospel of Matthew.* Grand Rapids, Mich.: Baker, 1973.

Holmes, Arthur F. *Ethics: Approaching Moral Decisions.* Downers Grove, Ill.: InterVarsity Press, 1984.

Jamieson, Robert, A. R. Fausset, and David Brown. *A Commentary, Critical, Experimental, and Practical, on the Old and New Testaments.* Grand Rapids, Mich.: Eerdmans, 1973.

John Wesley the Methodist. New York: Methodist Book Concern, 1903.

Johnston, Johanna. *Runaway to Heaven.* New York: Doubleday, 1963.

Lewis, C. S. *Mere Christianity.* New York: Macmillan, 1943.

Lloyd-Jones, Martin. *Studies in the Sermon on the Mount,* vol. 1. Grand Rapids, Mich.: Eerdmans, 1958.

MacArthur, John. *Matthew.* Chicago: Moody Press, 1968.

———. *Why Government Can't Save You.* Nashville: Word, 2000.

Marsden, George W. *Religion and American Culture.* Philadelphia: Harcourt Brace Jovanovich, 1990.

Mead, Frank S. *The March of Eleven Men.* New York: Grosset & Dunlap, 1931.

Merrill, Dean. *Sinners in the Hands of an Angry Church.* Grand Rapids, Mich.: Zondervan, 1997.

Parshall, Janet and Craig. *The Light in the City.* Nashville: Thomas Nelson Publishers, 2000.

Peterson, Eugene H. *The Message.* Colorado Springs, Colo.: NavPress, 1993.

Schaff, Philip. *History of the Christian Church.* Grand Rapids, Mich.: Eerdmans, 1921.

Schuckers, J. W. *The Life and Public Services of Salmon Portland Chase.* New York: Appleton, 1874.

Stewart, James Brewer. *Holy Warriors: The Abolitionists and American Slavery.* New York: Hill & Wang, 1976.

————. *Joshua R. Giddings and the Tactics of Radical Politics.* Cleveland: Press of Case Western Reserve University, 1970.

Stott, John R. W. *The Epistles of John.* Grand Rapids, Mich.: Eerdmans, 1976.

————. *The Message of the Sermon on the Mount (Matthew 5-7).* Downers Grove, Ill.: InterVarsity Press, 1978.

————. *Decisive Issues Facing Christians Today.* Old Tappan, N.J.: Revell, 1984.

Stowe, Harriet Beecher. *Uncle Tom's Cabin.* New York: Penguin Putnam, 1966.

Sweet, William W. *The Story of Religion in America.* Grand Rapids, Mich.: Baker, 1973.

Thomas, Benjamin P. *Theodore Weld, Crusader for Freedom.* New Brunswick, N.J.: Rutgers University Press, 1950.

Thomas, Cal, and Ed Dobson. *Blinded by Might.* Grand Rapids, Mich.: Zondervan, 1999.

Wagenknecht, Edward. *Harriet Beecher Stowe.* New York: Oxford University Press, 1965.

Wells, David F. *Losing Our Virtue.* Grand Rapids, Mich.: Eerdmans, 1998.

Wolters, Albert M. *Creation Regained: Biblical Basis for a Reformational World View.* Grand Rapids, Mich.: Eerdmans, 1985.

Yancey, Philip. *The Jesus I Never Knew.* Grand Rapids, Mich.: Zondervan, 1995.

Zodhiates, Spiros, ed. *The Complete Word Study Dictionary.* Chattanooga, Tenn.: AMG, 1992.

Articles

Arkes, Hadley. "Right to Choose, or License to Kill." *The Weekly Standard,* November 15, 1999, pp. 17-18.

Garbenis, Dean. "The Power of One." *Citizens' Courier* 18, no. 4 (winter 2000), p. 11.

Graham, Billy. "A Time for Moral Courage." *Reader's Digest,* July 1962, pp. 49-52.

Hess, Tom. "Uprising in Vermont." *Focus on the Family Citizen* 14, no. 12 (December 2000/January 2001), pp. 34-38.

Hooten, Jeff. "Living Proof." *Focus on the Family Citizen* 12, no. 10 (October 1998), pp. 18-21.

Mendenhall, Deborah. "Nightmarish Textbooks Await Your Kids." *Focus on the Family Citizen* 3, no. 9 (September 17, 1990), pp. 1-7.

Minnery, Tom. "Just a Little Bit of R-E-S-P-E-C-T." *Focus on the Family Citizen* 13, no. 2 (February 1999), p. 22.

Minnery, Tom. "So Long, *Sassy.*" *Focus on the Family Citizen* 11, no. 5 (May 26, 1997), p. 6.

Minnery, Tom. "Why the Gospel Grows in Socialist Nicaragua." *Christianity Today* 27, no. 7 (April 8, 1983), pp. 34-42.

Smith, Paul. "Mothers Fight a Sleazy Teen Magazine." *Focus on the Family Citizen* 2, no. 6 (July 1988), pp. 4-5.

United States Census data. Quoted in Paul Overberg. "Citizen Voting Rates Fall, Census Says." *USA Today,* July 19, 2000, p. 8A.

Will, George. "An Abortion Choice." *Washington Post,* November 24, 1996, p. C7.

SCRIPTURE REFERENCES

INDEX

FOCUS ON THE FAMILY®

Welcome to the *Family!*

Whether you received this book as a gift, borrowed it from
a friend, or purchased it yourself, we're glad you read it! It's just
one of the many helpful, insightful, and encouraging
resources produced by Focus on the Family.

In fact, that's what Focus on the Family is all about—providing inspiration, information, and biblically based advice to people in all stages of life.

It began in 1977 with the vision of one man, Dr. James Dobson, a licensed
psychologist and author of 16 best-selling books on marriage, parenting,
and family. Alarmed by the societal, political, and economic pressures
that were threatening the existence of the American family, Dr. Dobson
founded Focus on the Family with one employee—an assistant—
and a once-a-week radio broadcast, aired on only 36 stations.

Now an international organization, Focus on the Family is dedicated
to preserving Judeo-Christian values and strengthening the family
through more than 70 different ministries, including eight separate
daily radio broadcasts; television public service announcements;
13 publications; and a steady series of books and award-winning
films and videos for people of all ages and interests.

Recognizing the needs of, as well as the sacrifices and important
contributions made by, such diverse groups as educators, physicians,
attorneys, crisis pregnancy center staff, and single parents,
Focus on the Family offers specific outreaches to uphold and
minister to these individuals, too. And it's all done for one purpose,
and one purpose only: to encourage and strengthen individuals
and families through the life-changing message of Jesus Christ.

•   •   •

For more information about the ministry, or if we can be of help to your
family, simply write to Focus on the Family, Colorado Springs, CO 80995
or call 1-800-A-FAMILY (1-800-232-6459). Friends in Canada may write
Focus on the Family, P.O. Box 9800, Stn. Terminal, Vancouver, B.C. V6B 4G3.
or call 1-800-661-9800. Visit our Web site—www.family.org—
to learn more about Focus on the Family or to find out if
there is an associate office in your country.

We'd love to hear from you!

Recommended Resources
From Focus on the Family®!

Daily Citizen E-mail

Get the latest news on issues that affect you and your family with "CitizenLink." This complimentary e-mail service is delivered to you Monday through Friday with the latest news about cultural and spiritual trends, crucial legislation, and other important information. Commentary from Focus on the Family helps you put it all in perspective. A must for conservative Christians who want to stay in the loop!

To sign up for this complimentary e-mail service, visit
www.family.org/linkmail

CitizenLink Web Site

Be an informed citizen! "CitizenLink" is the place to go for answers to the hot-button issues affecting our country and culture. Insightful articles from *Citizen* magazine, research papers, online polls, analysis, and commentary are just a few of the many great resources you'll find to help you sort out the issues and bolster your convictions. Find out how you can make a difference as a citizen by logging on to: www.citizenlink.org

Citizen

Stay involved and up to the minute about politics, social issues, and much more! Each issue of *Citizen* magazine features hot-button topics, the latest in legislature, and articles from insiders who report what the mainstream media won't. Bold and thought-provoking, it's an information source no concerned citizen should be without!

Dietrich Bonhoeffer: The Cost of Freedom

When Hitler's Nazis rose to power in Germany, pastor and theologian Dietrich Bonhoeffer refused to take part in the evil. Eventually, Bonhoeffer's powerful faith became a threat to Hitler himself. Arrested for treason and deserted by his church, Bonhoeffer paid the ultimate price for his faith. In the exciting dramatization *Dietrich Bonhoeffer: The Cost of Freedom,* Focus on the Family Radio Theatre brings this unforgettable story to listeners who will find themselves challenged by the life and death of one of Christianity's greatest thinkers and most courageous souls.

• • •

Look for these special books in your Christian bookstore or request a copy by calling 1-800-A-FAMILY (1-800-232-6459). Friends in Canada may write to Focus on the Family, P.O. Box 9800, Stn. Terminal, Vancouver, B.C. V6B 4G3 or call 1-800-661-9800.

Visit our Web site (www.family.org) to learn more about the ministry or to find out if there is a Focus on the Family office in your country.